The Music Producer's Guide to Reverb

The Music Producer's Guide to Reverb

Published by Stereo Output Limited, company number 11174059

ISBN number 9781999600389

Please go to www.stereooutput.com to contact us or follow us on various social media channels.

Contents

Introduction

Reverb is one of the most vital effects in the music producer's repertoire. It can also be one of the most difficult to get right. A successful application of Reverb acts upon our innate perception of natural sound, and sometimes challenges it.

Natural reverb is one of the oldest musical effects in existence. Whether we're singing in the shower or busking in a shopping mall, the harmonics of our performance mix with the harmonics of the reflected sounds to create something special.

Reverb is built into many acoustic instruments by design. Hundreds of years of development have led to such innovations as the hollow chamber at the base of a hand drum or the resonating body of an acoustic guitar, giving the produced sound a rich character and unmistakable presence.

The music we create with the virtual instruments of a DAW, however, does not possess any of this vital acoustic information. It is the sonic equivalent of a two-dimensional image, instead of a three-dimensional object.

So how do we reconcile this disparity between our electronic music and the natural world?

How do we use an effects unit to alter our listeners' psychoacoustic perceptions and convey a physical environment?

How do we successfully harness something as simple as an echo to provide our music with unparalleled emotional and rhythmic power?

The answers to these questions lie within this book.

Chapter 1: The Basics of Signal Flow

Standard DAW applications, such as Ableton or Logic, provide the user with a broad range of virtual electronic devices. Some of these will be virtual instruments that function as sound producers. Others, such as samplers, will play back an audio file loaded into them. You will also encounter a third type of device, one designed for modifying an existing audio signal. These are known as *effects devices*.

Effects devices—such as reverb units—are integral to the process of modern music production and their mastery is crucial to creating music that meets today's high standards. It's essential to understand how effects devices change and transform the audio signal, since their incorrect placement can cause many undesirable outcomes, ranging from an unpleasant, unnatural sound to an incorrect mix.

To shape your sound with precision and avoid making rookie mistakes, it's worth taking a few moments at the outset of this book to investigate the subject of signal flow, so that once you deploy such devices within your DAW—as required in later Chapters—you will do so with complete confidence.

1.1: The Signal Flow

The term *signal flow* refers to the steps an audio signal has to pass through to get from the point at which it's generated to where it becomes audible sound. When you play a virtual synthesizer in your DAW, for example, the sound from your synthesizer must travel from the output of your plugin to become audio through your speakers. It does this through the signal flow.

Back in the day before computerised DAWs became standard, studio devices were linked to one another using cables that carried electrical signals, joining them together to form a chain. A cable would connect a microphone to a mixer, for example. Another would extend from the mixer to an amplifier, and a third would extend from the amp to the studio's speakers.

Reason's *Rack View* emulates the intricacy of old-school signal flow, as seen in Figure 1.1:

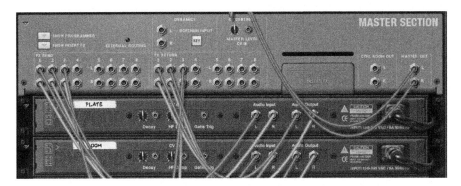

Figure 1.1: Reason's Rack View.

Today, we're dealing in the world of virtual signal flow. Fortunately, in most DAWs, the cabling is automatic, and the contemporary producer doesn't need to worry too much about the intricate connections between various devices. You will, however, need to keep a precise handle on the *direction* of the signal flow. This starts with the various sound-producing devices you're using. These will be routed through your mixer, where they will then converge upon the master output channel, as seen in Figure 1.2:

Figure 1.2: The basic signal flow within a DAW.

If you're using a DAW such as Ableton or Logic, your devices' output will go to the mixer, followed by the main output, unless routed otherwise.

Figure 1.3 shows this signal flow in Ableton. On the lower left, you can see the virtual instrument, in this case a bass synthesizer.

Signals from this synthesizer route into Channel 2 of the mixer, which, along with the other mixer channels, converge upon the output channel seen in the top-right:

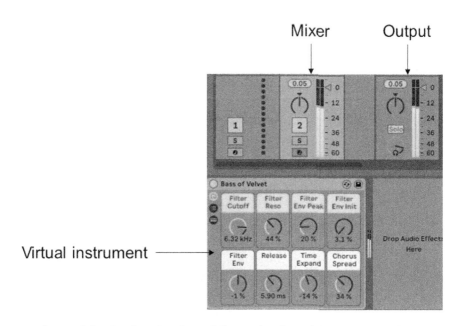

Figure 1.3: The basic signal flow, depicted in Ableton Live.

It is at this point that we will want to change the quality of our sound, using an effects plugin. There are three ways to do this. You can use *Insert Effects*, *Bus Effects* and/or *Aux Effects*.

1.2: Insert Effects

At the simplest level, we would add our effects plugin *between* the virtual instrument and the mixer. This means you will affect the sound from your instrument after it has been created, but before it enters the mixer and subsequent output channel.

You can do this in Ableton by dropping it to the right of the instrument, creating the signal flow shown in Figure 1.4:

Figure 1.4: The signal flow with an insert effect added.

Such a signal flow is shown in Figure 1.5, again using Ableton:

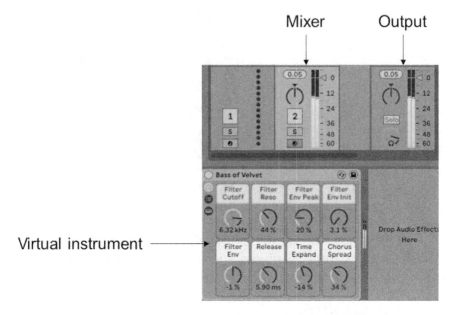

Figure 1.5: An Insert Effect signal flow in Ableton Live.

In Logic, you can add an Insert Effect under the instrument in the channel strip, as shown in Figure 1.6:

Figure 1.6: An Insert Effect in Logic.

You are not limited to a single Insert Effect, of course. You can add multiple effects units to create an effects 'chain', as illustrated in Figure 1.7:

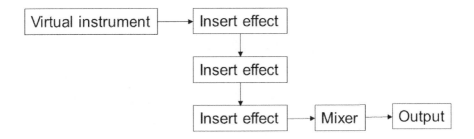

Figure 1.7: An effects chain.

Creating an effects chain in Ableton is as easy as adding further effects units to the right of your instrument.

In Logic, you would continue adding them under your first effects unit.

Remember that the order of these effects unit matters, so in Ableton, an effects unit to the right of another will process the output of the unit to its immediate left. An example is shown in Figure 1.8:

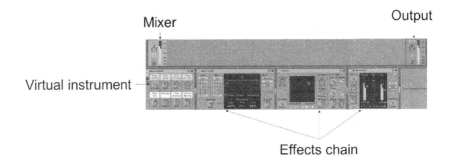

Figure 1.8: An effects chain in Ableton Live. The 'chain' is created by effects units to the right of others in the channel.

In Logic, meanwhile, an effects unit processes the output of whatever is above it, as shown in Figure 1.9:

Figure 1.9: The Chroma Reverb is added to the output of the Noise Gate.

If you wanted to send the output of many tracks through *the same insert effect*, you would use the second type of approach: a bus track.

1.3: Bus Effects

A bus is a mixer track that contains a sum of other mixer tracks. It accepts signals being sent to it from other tracks, but you cannot record onto it.

Some producers like to send all their mixer channels of a similar type to a bus. They might, for example, send all their drums or all their synthesizer channels. By routing several mixer tracks to a single bus, you can then add an effect on to that bus, and the effect will subsequently act on all the channels routed through it— this is called a *bus effect*.

This is illustrated in Figure 1.10:

affected by the reflective and absorptive properties of the materials present.

To illustrate this, try the following experiment. First, clap your hands in your living room, and listen to the reverberation of the sound. Next, do the same in your bathroom. You will probably notice how the reverberation in the bathroom is louder and more persistent (which is what makes it such an ideal space for singing).

The difference in the reverberations being generated in these two respective rooms is because of the contrasting properties of the surfaces within them. Whereas your living room will contain more absorptive objects, such as curtains, chairs, carpets and rugs, your bathroom will probably have more hard surfaces such as ceramic tiles and smooth walls.

2.1: Transmission, Reflection, and Absorption of Sound

Sound propagates as a wave that travels through a medium, such as a liquid, a solid or a gas (like the surrounding air). It causes the molecules of that medium to vibrate, pushing and pulling against those next to them, as the sound wave moves outward from its source.

Just like light waves, when sound waves encounter a surface, three things will happen to different extents:

> 1. Transmission—some of the sound waves move through the object to whatever sits behind.

> 2. Reflection—some of the sound waves bounce off the object, creating echoes.

> 3. Absorption—some of the sound waves get 'trapped' by the object itself, where their energy is transformed into a small amount of heat. This is also known as conversion.

These three are shown in Figure 2.1:

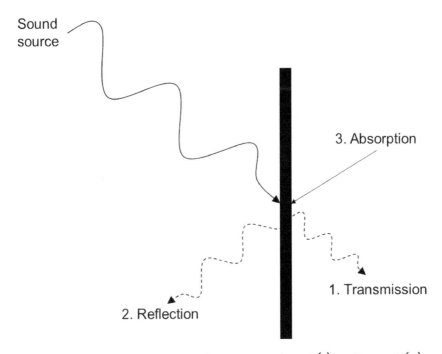

Sound source

3. Absorption

1. Transmission

2. Reflection

Figure 2.1: A sound wave being transmitted (1), reflected (2) and absorbed (3).

Usually, a combination of all three events takes place. The degree of each depends on the material composition of the object and the range of frequencies of the original sound waves, whether these are low frequencies—like the rumbling of a passing train—or high frequencies, such as a car alarm.

Hard surfaces are more reflective than soft surfaces. Thicker or more dense objects are more absorptive. Conversely, thinner, or less dense objects are more transmissive.

Low-frequency sounds are more likely to be transmitted, whilst high-frequency sounds are more likely to be reflected or absorbed. This is because higher frequencies lose energy faster than lower frequencies when they encounter a solid object. It is for this reason that you're more likely to hear the bass of your neighbour's music through the walls than you are the treble.

When studying absorption, we need to look at it across several frequencies. A material's absorptive property may be expressed by a sound absorption coefficient, α. This will measure how much of a sound is transmitted or absorbed/converted into heat.

As Table 2.1 shows, different materials have different absorption coefficients. A higher value means more absorption; fibreglass, for example, is more absorptive than brick.

Table 2.1: The absorption coefficients of various materials at a range of frequencies.

Material	125 Hz	250 Hz	500 Hz	1 kHz	2 kHz	4 kHz	Average
Brick (natural)	0.03	0.03	0.03	0.04	0.05	0.07	**0.04**
Brick (painted)	0.01	0.01	0.02	0.02	0.02	0.03	**0.02**
Carpet	0.01	0.02	0.06	0.15	0.25	0.45	**0.16**
Concrete (sealed or painted)	0.01	0.01	0.02	0.02	0.02	0.02	**0.02**
Concrete block (coarse)	0.36	0.44	0.31	0.29	0.39	0.25	**0.34**
Concrete block (painted)	0.1	0.05	0.06	0.07	0.09	0.08	**0.08**
Fibreglass board (100mm(4″) thick)	0.99	0.99	0.99	0.99	0.99	0.97	**0.99**
Glass (small pane)	0.04	0.04	0.03	0.03	0.02	0.02	**0.03**
Marble or glazed tile	0.01	0.01	0.01	0.01	0.02	0.02	**0.01**
Snow	0.08	0.2	0.45	0.9	0.85	0.75	**0.54**
Water surface	0.01	0.01	0.01	0.01	0.02	0.02	**0.01**
Wood flooring on joists	0.15	0.11	0.1	0.07	0.06	0.07	**0.09**

Looking at average absorption coefficients in more detail in Table 2.1, we can see huge differences in how absorptive different materials can be. Water has an average absorption coefficient of 0.01, unless it falls as snow, in which case it is fifty times more absorptive, which is why—traffic disruption aside—the world often seems so much quieter under a blanket of snow. A concrete block is highly absorptive, unless you paint it, in which case its absorption coefficient is quartered, as the smoother surface now reflects more of the sound wave.

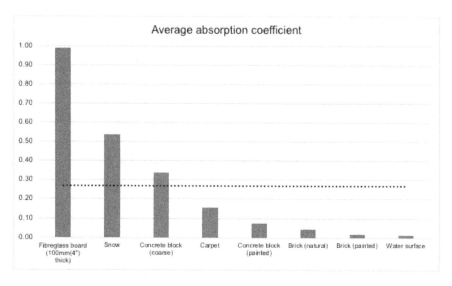

Figure 2.2: The average absorption coefficients of various materials.

Visualising this as a graph in Figure 2.2 above, we can see the extent to which the average absorption coefficient of various materials deviate from the average (the dotted line).

We can explore this further by comparing how absorptive three different materials are at different frequencies, as shown in Figure 2.3:

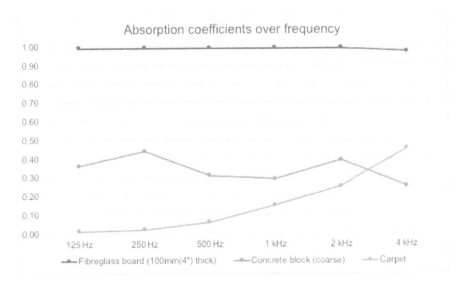

Figure 2.3: The average absorption coefficients over frequency of three materials.

As you can see, thick fibreglass board is consistently absorptive regardless of frequency, whilst a concrete block's absorption coefficient varies depending on frequency. Carpet is moderately absorptive at higher frequencies, but not at all absorptive at lower frequencies.

By relating the above information to your own experience gained from attentive listening, you can begin to understand the contrasting sonic properties of many environments, from the tremendous reverberation present in spaces such as cathedrals and vast caverns, to the dull lack of reverberation in your warm, musty attic.

The reason many of our musical instruments—and even our own voices—harness natural reverb so well is because they often occupy middling frequencies, and therefore sit in the sweet spot of the absorption coefficient curve. Lower frequencies don't get absorbed as they are usually transmitted instead, and higher frequencies are easily absorbed.

Remember also that absorption is only one of three things that happen when sound waves reach a material: any sound that isn't absorbed will be transmitted and reflected.

The most important points to remember are:

- Reverberation depends on the materials present within the environment.

- Different materials vary in their absorption coefficient, not just in terms of their absorptive capacity, but their absorptive capacity over different frequencies.

- Audible reflections are biased towards the middling frequency range. The lower the sound, the more likely it is to be transmitted; the higher the sound, the more likely it will be absorbed.

Now let's look at sonic reflections themselves and their role in creating reverberations.

2.2: Reverberations

When a sound occurs, sound waves radiate outwards in all directions and reverberate from the surrounding surfaces. A listener will hear a combination of the direct sound from the source, reflections from these surfaces, and subsequent reflections of the reflections themselves. These reflections continue until all the sound has been absorbed or transmitted.

As an analogy, imagine dropping a stone into a still bucket of water. Initially, the ripples on the surface will radiate outwards from the point where you dropped the stone, but as these ripples

of this space, sound waves would arrive at the walls more quickly. Because there are only six surfaces—four walls, plus floor and ceiling—the reflections would be less diffuse in their direction and the fibreglass would absorb much of the sound that arrives at it, as shown in Figure 2.5:

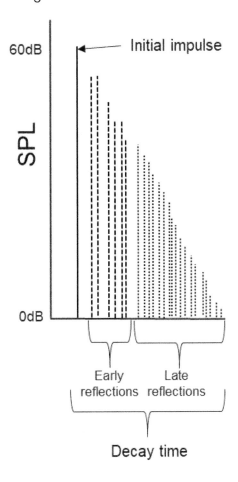

Figure 2.5: The hypothetical impulse response of a small rectangular room insulated by fibreglass.

Compare this to a large room in the shape of an irregular octagon, with walls of painted concrete. Because of the greater size of this space, the sound waves would take longer to bounce.

The reflections would be more diffuse since there are many more surfaces for them to bounce off. More of each reflection would continue to be reflected because of the painted concrete surfaces. The combination of these factors would create a long reverberation tail that would sound 'smeared' because of the attributes of this room, as seen in Figure 2.6:

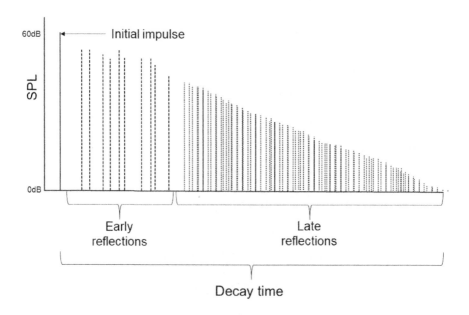

Figure 2.6: The hypothetical impulse response of a large, irregular octagonal room with painted concrete walls.

These charts are merely a representation of overall sound pressure level; in reality, each frequency will have a slightly different reverb tail. The most important consideration is *how the high frequencies behave*. In a room with softer surfaces, reverb tails will lose high frequencies as they bounce around. The character of the reverb tail will therefore show a greater change over time than those shown in the impulse response charts above.

Figure 2.7 for example, displays the reverb tail that results when we measure the tail of a single middling frequency and a single high frequency:

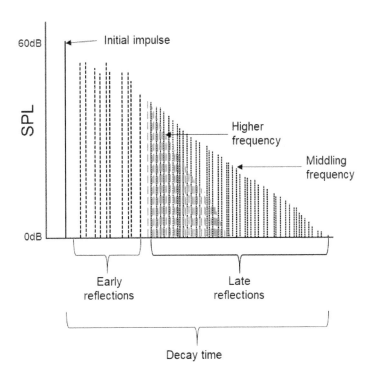

Figure 2.7: The hypothetical impulse responses of a single middling frequency and a single high frequency.

To summarise this chapter, how sound reflections behave in a space will depend on several factors:

- The size of the room.

- The shape of the room.

- The surfaces of the room.

These reflections can be split into two distinct stages: early reflections and late reflections. Together, these two stages comprise the reverb tail. The reverb tail is measured by the time it takes for the sound to decay by 60dB, which is 1/1000th of its original level. To simulate reverberation as a musical effect, all the above factors must be part of the simulation.

Chapter 3: The History of Reverb

3.1: Acoustics

People have been harnessing the power of reverberation since ancient times. There is plenty of evidence to show that our forebears enjoyed echoes and reverberations every bit much as we do today and were acutely aware of their power to transform ordinary sound into something that could evoke feelings of awe and mystery. It's no coincidence that cave paintings are often found in the most reverberant sections of the cavern.

A recent study by the University of Salford suggests that the 4500-year-old stone circles of Stonehenge were constructed in ways that would have increased the volume of the human voice by four decibels in the interior, whilst excluding exterior noise. Any music performed inside the monument itself would have produced strong reverberations from the reflective surfaces of the enormous stones surrounding the performers themselves. One can only imagine the intensity of the atmosphere created by rituals held there.

Historic theatres, cathedrals, and temples in both the East and the West were designed to optimise acoustics. The amphitheatres of ancient Greece and Rome, for example, exploited reverberation to ensure that every member of the audience could hear the performers with clarity, thanks to the reflective nature of their stone seating.

In Figure 3.1, we can see the remains of the amphitheatre built at Delphi around 400 BC:

Figure 3.1: A 4th century BC amphitheatre at Delphi.

In China, the courtyard theatres dating from the Ming Dynasty onwards featured innovations such as a domed ceiling and a curved space at the back of the courtyard to reflect sound to the audience. Similarly, the theatres of the European Renaissance often employed curved seating areas, akin to those of the ancient Greece and Rome.

Images of both are shown in Figure 3.2.

Figure 3.3: Columbia's 30th Street Studio.

Studios on a tight budget meanwhile would use echo rooms. These were often the most reverberant area the technicians could find, such as the studio bathroom or the building's stairwell. Music producers would play their recordings through a loudspeaker into a microphone, pick up the area's natural reverberation and then combine this reverberated sound with the original recording.

This technique—of adding desirable reverb whilst controlling the amount present—was pioneered in 1947 by Bill Putnam Sr., who used the studio's bathroom as an echo chamber on the Harmonicats' *Peg O' My Heart*. Using the most reverberant rooms available was a great way to add reverb to recordings at minimal cost, although it had its downsides when someone flushing a toilet interrupted a take!

Studios with bigger budgets meanwhile, began developing dedicated *echo chambers*. These were hollow rooms, often built out into underground space below the studio building. They were designed for optimal reverberation, were often of a non-parallel shape (to keep the reverberations smooth) and made use of highly reverberant surfaces like concrete, or multiple layers of drywall.

An example of an echo room is shown in Figure 3.4:

Figure 3.4: An echo chamber.

Echo chambers soon became the established way for many studios to add reverb to their recordings. Producers could capture alternative reverb takes by altering the positioning of the microphone or speakers: aiming the speaker towards a wall, for example, or placing multiple microphones in different parts of the echo chamber.

Such echo chambers possessed unique sonic characteristics. Because of the small sizes of such rooms, the resulting reverberations were quite dense. The decay time was much shorter at higher frequencies than at lower ones, to the extent that at Abbey Road studios it was common to use an equaliser to filter out recorded reverb frequencies below 600Hz and above 10kHz.

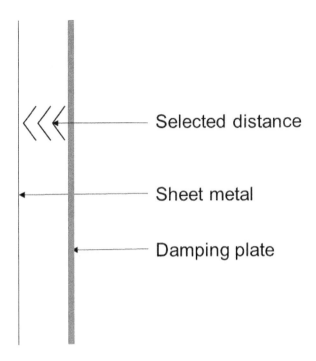

Figure 3.8: The damping of plate reverb using a damping plate.

The EMT 140's sound was revered, and its reputation was further enhanced in 1961 when EMT added an additional pickup for a stereo signal return, giving producers the opportunity to create more realistic simulated spaces. By the 1970s, EMT had also updated the tube circuitry to take advantage of solid-state transistors that were more dependable than their tube counterparts, adding to the unit's prestige.

3.4: Digital reverb

Alongside the creation of these mechanical reverberation units, work began during the early 1960s to develop reverb algorithms that computers could use to simulate reverb.

Since reverberations are copies of an original sound, the first requirement of a reverb algorithm was that it should be able to produce multiple, delayed duplicates of a sound. The second requirement was that this cascade of echoes would decay in volume over time, just like real reverberations.

In a famous paper published in 1962 called *Natural Sounding Artificial Reverberation*, German physicist Manfred Schroeder hypothesised that to sound natural, a minimum of 1,000 echoes per second would be required.

Together with American electrical engineer Ben Logan, Schroeder pioneered artificial reverberation by using multiple comb filters, which created slightly delayed copies of the sound in parallel.

These delays could be fed back into the input, with a slight reduction in gain in each loop (by setting the gain just below 1), as shown in Figure 3.9:

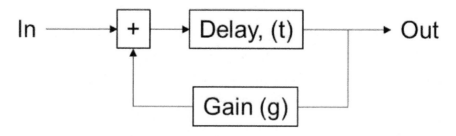

Figure 3.9: The schematic of a feedback loop. Recreated and adapted from "Colorless" Artificial Reverberation (Schroeder and Logan, 1961).

This would create an impulse response that decayed over time, somewhat resembling natural reverberation, as shown in Figure 3.10:

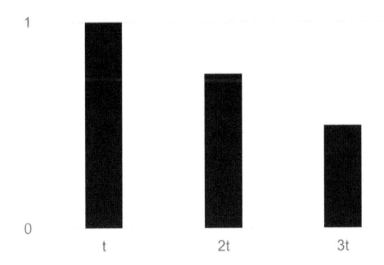

Figure 3.10: The impulse response generated by the feedback loop. Recreated and adapted from "Colorless" Artificial Reverberation (Schroeder and Logan, 1961).

The key problem with this approach was that the results lacked essential realism; unlike the smudged sound of genuine reverberation, these copies sounded too uniform, too perfect.

The solution was to mix some of the original sound with the echoes. This sounded far more lifelike, and the resulting system was termed an all-pass delay, as depicted in Figure 3.11:

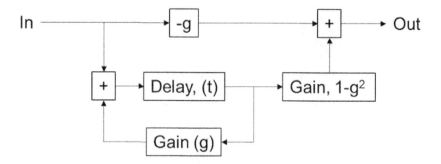

Figure 3.11: The layout of an all-pass delay. Recreated and adapted from "Colorless" Artificial Reverberation (Schroeder and Logan, 1961).

It was termed an all-pass delay because it passed all frequencies equally (unlike a low-pass or high-pass) and therefore had the same frequency response as its input.

One difficulty with this system, however, was that the delays still arrived at a constant rate and with a constant frequency response. This caused several issues with the realism of the reverb tail, because:

- Real-life reverberations are not equally spaced out.

- There are significant variations in intensity between real-life reflections.

- Real-life reverberations become more diffuse as the reverb tail decays.

Schroeder therefore proposed spreading the delay times of these comb filters out.

To mitigate the potential for these delays to 'bunch' together in undesirable ways, the delay time for each comb filter was set to a relatively prime value, so that when multiplied, the delay times didn't create common values.

Additional thickening of the sound was achieved by passing the signal from the comb filters into two all-pass filters in series, as shown in Figure 3.12. These all-pass filters altered the phase of varying frequencies, creating additional 'smearing', and preventing the echoes from destructively interfering with one another:

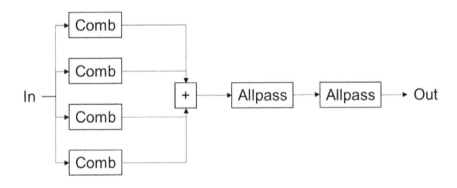

Figure 3.12: The schematic of Schroeder's reverberator.

Schroeder further suggested values for each loop delay time that would be appropriate for simulating various real-life scenarios, such as the concert hall shown in Table 3.1:

Table 3.1: The suggested loop time intervals for a concert hall setting of the distinct elements of Schroeder's reverberator.

Element	Loop time (ms)
Comb filter 1	29.7
Comb filter 2	37.1
Comb filter 3	41.1
Comb filter 4	43.7
Allpass filter 1	5.0
Allpass filter 2	1.7

Although created using rather esoteric means, these algorithms became the basis for modern digital reverb. They are still in use— in some shape or form—even to this day.

The study of this history is useful for the music producer because it shows us that the development of digital reverb involved five key factors:

1. The creation of repetitions of the source sound.

2. The 'decay' of these repetitions over time.

3. The spacing of these repetitions, using prime values so that they don't bunch together.

4. The altering of the phase of these repetitions to reduce the extent to which they interfere with one another.

5. The mixing of the original signal with these repetitions.

Based on further iteration and development of Schroeder's algorithms, EMT and other manufacturers (such as Lexicon) developed digital reverb units which first began appearing on the market in the mid-1970s. One of the most successful examples of these was the floor-standing EMT 250 Electronic Reverberator Unit, as shown in Figure 3.13:

Figure 3.13: The EMT 250 Electronic Reverberator Unit.

Its use of software signalled the future of music production.

Because the algorithms used were based around copies of the input sound, the EMT 250 could offer delay, echo, chorus, and phaser effects in addition to reverb. That these distinct effects could now be added to a single reverberation unit based on their algorithmic similarity greatly increased this unit's marketability.

Akin to the EMT 140 plate reverb, the EMT 250 could create reverb decays from 0.4s to 4.5s and even offered an additional 'Space Mode' that generated a reverb with a fixed decay of 10 seconds. Its low computing power however meant that it had lower sampling rates than today's hardware and software and was unable to output reverb above 10kHz.

An alternative reverb unit, the Lexicon 224, shown in Figure 3.14, was released in 1979. Smaller than the EMT 250, it employed similar algorithms:

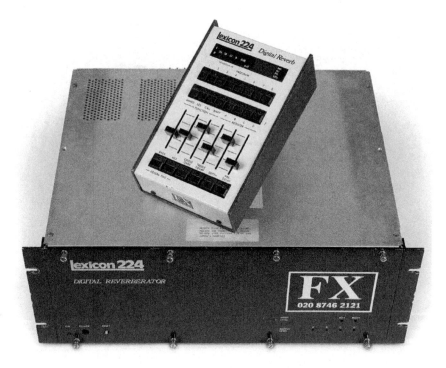

Figure 3.14: The Lexicon 224.

The Lexicon 224 could generate extremely long decay times of up to 70 seconds, which far exceeded those available in nature. This paved the way for the additional use of reverb as a purely creative element within modern musical recordings.

In the late 1970s, American digital audio engineer James A. Moorer improved on Schroeder's design to arrive at a reverb algorithm called Moorer's Reverberator. This simulated not only a reverb tail but also the early reflections stage of reverberation. Sounds that entered Moorer's Reverberator initially travelled through a network of delays, simulating early reflections. This signal was subsequently passed to parallel comb filters, with different delay lengths to simulate the reverb tail. To mimic the absorption of higher frequencies by air, Moorer added low-pass filters to the feedback loop, as shown in Figure 3.15:

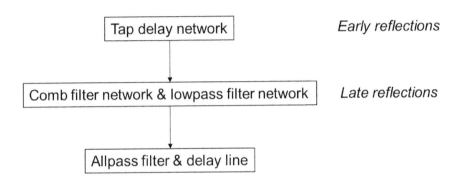

Figure 3.15: The basic method of Moorer's Reverberator.

The 1980s saw the release of many digital reverbs that built upon Moorer's work, such as the Lexicon 224XL, AMS RMX16 and the Klark Teknik DN780, to name but a few.

These machines offered a vast number of different algorithms, some of which were well outside natural reverberation. Such algorithms included:

- Reverse reverbs, that sounded like a reverb recorded and played backwards.

- Gated reverb, where a reverb tail was abruptly truncated.

- Shimmer, where a reverb would move upward in pitch as it decayed.

As computers became more advanced through the 1990s, so digital reverb became more powerful. Exponentially increasing processing power meant that highly developed algorithms could be used, with more intricate modelling of early reflections and greater memory available for a detailed reverb tail. It was around this time that Moorer and Schroeder's previous work on reverb algorithms became the basis for a new concept called *Feedback Delay Networks.*

A Feedback Delay Network is an umbrella term for many ways of simulating reverberation, but the fundamental concept is that delays are cross coupled; in other words, they are fed into one another, to mix with each other. This not only allows for a smoother reverb tail but also a better interaction between individual echoes, thus simulating reverberation with greater realism. The complexity of a Feedback Delay Network also provides for improved control of time-dependent frequency response, (the interaction between early and late reflections) as shown in Figure 3.16:

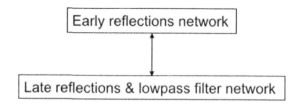

Figure 3.16: The interaction between the early reflections network and the late reflections & low-pass filter network.

Around the turn of the Millennium, an alternative method for creating digital reverberation was released: *convolution reverb.* Although previously theorised, there had never been sufficient processing power available at a low enough cost to make convolution reverb commercially viable. By 1999, however, the situation had significantly improved and mass-produced units such as the Sony DRE S777 had become available for purchase.

Unlike the digital units of the time, which allowed users to set the parameters of the artificial reverb within the unit, the DRE S777 gave users the opportunity to select from real-life spaces, such as famous concert halls, music studios or cathedrals. It even allowed the user—if they possessed the required technology—to sample reverberant spaces for themselves.

The premise underlying convolution reverb was simple. As already discussed, acoustic spaces possess different reverberant properties to one another. In convolution reverb, the profile of how a particular space responds to a sound is mapped to build its entire impulse response, meaning that the way sounds reverberate within it can be modelled. A convolution reverb unit would therefore be able to simulate Boston's Symphony Hall, or Abbey Road's Studio 2 echo chamber, at little cost to the consumer.

Convolution reverb involved a substantial amount of initial work because the impulse response of each environment had to be captured. At its most basic level, this required an accurate speaker and microphone. An impulse would be sounded, such as a white noise pulse, or a sine wave sweeping from 20Hz to 20kHz, and the microphone would capture the reverberation, as depicted in Figure 3.17:

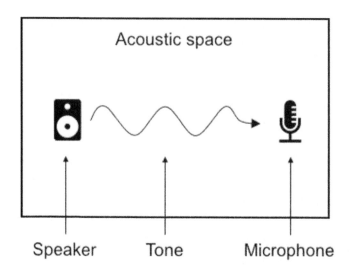

Figure 3.17: The basic layout of an impulse response capture.

Once the original impulse had been eliminated from the
recordings through a process called deconvolution, this response
would provide a model of the reverberation at each frequency
over time, resulting in an impulse response such as the one
depicted in Figure 3.18:

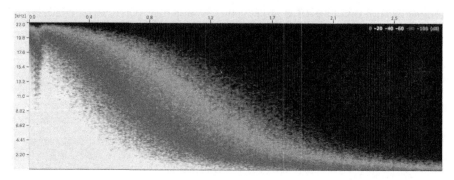

Figure 3.18: The captured impulse response of a space.

By placing microphones in many areas of a room, it was possible
to not only simulate an established acoustic space but also the
reverberation that could be expected from any location inside it,
with an extraordinary degree of accuracy.

Convolution reverb was a revolutionary innovation for producers on low budgets who were digitally composing orchestral music. Rather than endlessly tweak algorithmic reverbs, they could now load a file containing the impulse response of an orchestral chamber and the artificial reverb would be difficult to distinguish from a real recording made in that environment.

Impulse responses were not limited to reverberant spaces alone. The impulse response of a spring reverb or even a delay unit could be recorded. This meant that convolution could simulate both actual spaces and the unique characteristics of effects devices themselves. One could even create a fictional space by synthesizing its impulse response.

As with many other technologies, the reduced cost of computing power has revolutionised simulating reverberation and the practice of improving it continues to this day.

Nowadays, good quality reverbs—whether algorithmic or convolution—come packaged free within most DAW software. And like many contemporary musical tools, something designed to simulate reality at a lesser cost has itself become a source for creative innovation. Artificial reverb is not only used to make music sound more natural and pleasurable, but also to contrive original soundscapes that bear no resemblance to acoustic reality.

Chapter 4: Common Reverb Functions

Having investigated the history of artificial reverb, it's now time to delve into how it works within a contemporary context, beginning with the common primary functions that one would expect to find on a standard digital reverb device.

Reverb devices differ from plugin to plugin, often more so than delays or compressors. When dealing with reverb terminology therefore, it's important to know that there can often be crossovers between terms, and that similar functions can be given different names, all depending on the unit. This can make things tricky. The important aspect to remember is that reverberation effects are usually modelled on real-world reverberation. Because of this, most reverb plugins will offer you control of the following key parameters:

- The equalisation and shape of the impulse response

- The size, shape, or surface of the reflective environment.

- The dynamics of the early reflections and how they feed into the late reflection tail.

- The equalisation, shape, and stereo image of the reverb tail.

We'll therefore begin by looking at the most common way plugins give you control of these essential parameters, a fundamental understanding of which will then enable you to glide more easily between different reverb plugins.

4.1: Dry/Wet

Dry/Wet, sometimes known as Depth, is a function on many effects units, shown here in Ableton, Figure 4.1:

Figure 4.1: The Dry/Wet function on Ableton Live's Reverb.

Dry/Wet allows you to specify how much of the audio signal you wish to be processed by the reverb unit:

- 100% Wet is the reverberated signal in its entirety.

- 50% Wet is a 50/50 mix of the reverberated (Wet) and non-reverberated (Dry) signals.

- 0% Wet (or 100% Dry) means none of the reverberated signal comes through the output.

This is illustrated in Figure 4.2:

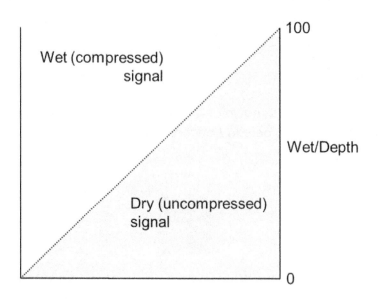

100

Wet (compressed) signal

Wet/Depth

Dry (uncompressed) signal

0

Figure 4.2: An illustration of how Wet/Dry works.

Depending on the proportion of Dry and Wet, a sound can seem to be close or distant. Even in a reflective environment, a sound directly in front of you will naturally be drier than one occurring farther away. This is because the closer you are to the source, the more of the direct sound you hear in comparison with the reverberated sound.

Instead of a Dry/Wet scale, some units allow Dry and Wet to be independently selected, as seen in Logic Pro X, Figure 4.3:

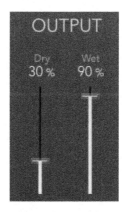

Figure 4.3: Independent Dry/Wet sliders.

Don't let this confuse you! The effect of using two sliders is the same as using one. What differs is how you achieve that effect.

When using two sliders that move independently, it is the ratio between the two values that matters, as shown in the 30%/90% setting in Figure 4.3 above. Although it might not seem immediately apparent, this is the same as using 75% Wet on a single slider, because 30 + 90 = 120.

30 is 1/4 of 120, which equates to 25% Wet.

25% Dry and 25% Wet will therefore sound the same as 100% Dry plus 100% Wet – the only difference will be in the amplitude.

4.2: Pre-delay

Pre-delay is the time that elapses between the direct sound and the start of the early reflections. Like the RT60, pre-delay conveys information about the environment. The larger the space, the longer the time it takes for sound to travel to the reflective boundaries (such as the walls of a room) and back to the listener.

Pre-delay also tells the listener about the distance between the source and themselves; the closer one's proximity to the source, the longer the pre-delay. This is because the relative distance between the direct and reflected sounds reduces as the source becomes farther from the listener, as shown in Figure 4.4:

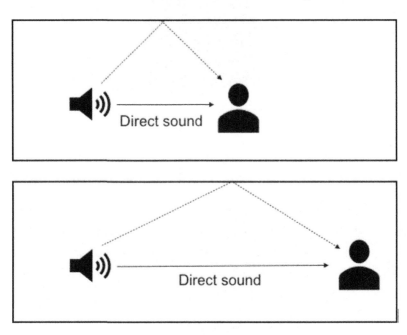

Figure 4.4: Pre-delay in two different rooms.

The pre-delay for natural sound is usually between 1ms and 25ms, although some reverb units offer a pre-delay of up to one second.

For those who love to design unique sonic environments, long pre-delay times can create some fascinating effects; imagine a reverberation that doesn't begin until the next note has been struck, for example.

4.3: Early Reflections

As discussed in Chapter 2, early reflections are the first reflections to arrive at the listener. These are highlighted in Figure 4.5:

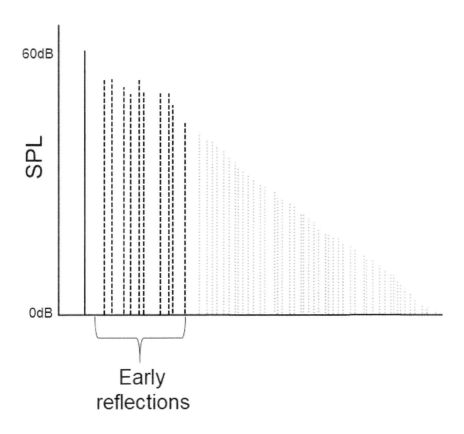

Figure 4.5: A reverb tail, with early reflections highlighted.

Early reflections bounce from only a few surfaces. They arrive a few milliseconds apart from one another and generally within the first 100ms following the direct sound. It is on this basis that our brain correlates them with the original signal and uses them to provide us with valuable data about the acoustic space. Accurate early reflections are therefore vital for correct simulation of reverberation.

The level of early reflections suggests the size of the environment, with larger environments creating quieter early reflections that take longer to arrive. A reflective environment will provide louder early reflections than a non-reflective one.

Many reverb plugins offer the option to sculpt early reflections to your preferences—this process usually involves configuring the amplitude, modulation, and frequency range of the early reflections:

- Amplitude or level allows you to control the intensity of the early reflections. A low intensity of early reflections conveys the impression of a sound that's arriving from a distance— although it should be noted that an extremely low intensity can sound unrealistic.

- Modulation allows you to simulate the chorusing effect that occurs when the early reflections mix with each other. A low frequency simulates a lower reflection density, and a higher frequency simulates a higher frequency density. A Dry/Wet control lets you simulate the extent of this modulation, where a drier sound will simulate a smaller space and a wetter one a larger space.

- Filters enable you to remove lower frequencies to prevent your reverberations from being too muddy. They can also remove higher frequencies to simulate absorptive materials such as carpet.

- Send (known as Shape in Ableton) gives you control over the extent to which the early reflections are fed into the later reverb tail. A good algorithmic reverb can create a smooth transition from the early reflections into the reverb tail.

4.4: Reverb Time

Reverb Time refers to the RT60 of the reverb (the time it takes for the reverb to decay to 1/1000th of its peak). Some plugins focus on the peak of the direct sound, whilst others address the peak of the first early reflection. For most practical purposes, the distinction doesn't matter much, as you will tweak this parameter according to what sounds right to you.

The decay time gives your listener information about the room, both in terms of its size and the reflectivity of the materials within it. The RT60 of a small absorbent room will usually be around 200ms, whilst a huge reverberant hall could have an RT60 lasting 8 seconds.

Longer decay creates a heavier atmosphere where one note may blur into the next, whereas a shorter decay creates a tighter atmosphere that more clearly preserves the distinction between the notes. Too long a decay, and the instruments can sound washed out. Too short a decay, and the reverb can sap the power of the instrument adding no significant atmosphere.

Remember that RT60 only defines the *length* of the reverb tail, not the *shape*—the two reverb tails illustrated in Figure 4.6 will sound different, despite having the same RT60. The reverb tail on the left has a sparser early reflections section, and decays linearly. It will therefore sound smoother, but hollower. The reverb tail on the right has a denser set of early reflections, but decays in a more exponential manner, before gradually fading at the end. This will sound more sudden and choppier:

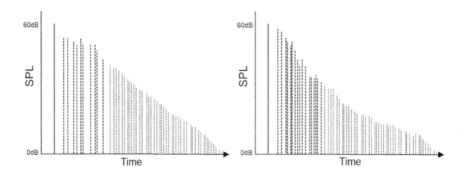

Figure 4.6: Two comparable reverb tails. Even though their duration is the same, their shape is unique.

Remember also that RT60 defines the time it takes for the reverberation to reduce by 60dB. Although this is a long way to drop, it's important to remember within the context of a mix—particularly with other elements playing—the audible time of a reverb tail will always be far less than its configured RT60, and after dropping by only 30dB it may cease to be audible altogether. Therefore, although you may program a three-second RT60 into your reverb plugin, this won't always result in three seconds of audible reverb tail.

4.5: Density & Diffusion

Density and diffusion can behave similarly to one another, although the way each are simulated is slightly different. Confusingly, the terms density and diffusion may also be used interchangeably, depending on the algorithm employed.

Density refers to the 'thickness' of the reverb tail. This can be because of the number of echoes that occur within it, the distance between the early reflections and later reverb tail and sometimes a combination of the two. Density can control early reflections alone, the reverb tail alone, or both—it all depends on the algorithm used.

A relatively dense reverb tail leads to a proliferation of echoes squeezed into the RT60 period. This produces a fairly smooth reverb tail.

A lower early reflection density can minimise any artefacts caused by interactions between the initial impulse and the subsequent crossover. High early reflection density can create a reverb tail that is often smoother overall, as the different early reflection echoes will blur together within it.

Lower reverb tail densities are helpful on slow sounds like pads, as they help maintain the clarity of the pad's sound. Higher reverb tail densities meanwhile will be helpful on sounds with more transients—such as drums whose characteristically sharp attack can lead to a 'fluttering' sound if the number of early reflections is too few.

Diffusion defines how the reverb tail is scattered around the hypothetical space. A highly diffused space will have more surfaces to bounce off and there will be a higher number of echoes, resulting in a smooth reverb tail. Depending on the plugin and algorithm used, diffusion can affect both early reflections and the reverb tail itself.

In real-life environments, diffusion is affected by both the regularity of a room shape and its surface properties. Irregular room shapes with more randomly angled surfaces will increase the degree of diffusion.

The two densities are compared in Figure 4.7 and Figure 4.8:

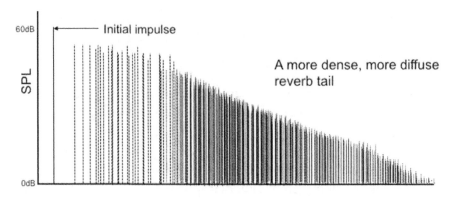

Figure 4.7: More dense, more diffuse reverb tail.

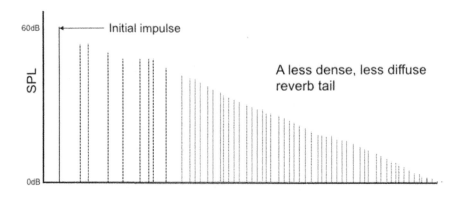

Figure 4.8: Less dense, less diffuse reverb tail.

As you can see, a more dense, more diffuse reverb tail includes many more reflections over the course of the reverb tail, leading to a perception of a smoother reverb tail.

In summary, greater density and diffusion create a smoother reverb tail.

4.6: Damping & Filtering

One of the most critical aspects of the reverberant response of a space is how the frequency response of a reverb tail changes through time. As we saw in Chapter 2, many materials absorb different amounts of sound depending upon the sound's frequency, for example snow, which absorbs very little low-frequency content but lots of middle and high frequency content. It is therefore important that a simulation of reverb accounts for this. Excess low or high frequency content within a reverb tail can sound bad in a mix, so it's paramount for a reverb device to filter this content.

A reverb tail with more high frequency content will imply a smaller space and/or more reflective surfaces. Conversely, a rapid loss of high frequency content suggests a larger space and/or more absorptive surfaces.

The three principal ways to alter the frequency response are:

- Equalisation before the sound is reverberated.

- Equalisation of the reverb tail.

- Damping.

Equalisation before the sound is reverberated is often accomplished using a band-pass filter at the first stage of the signal flow through the reverb device. This allows the user to select the pass-through band. This is often used when there are frequencies within the input signal that the producer doesn't want reverberated. Two good examples of this are:

- Low bass tones, that could make the reverb tail sound muddy.

- Very high frequency percussion, that could make the reverb tail sound tinny.

Removing these undesired frequencies can often make the reverb sound much clearer and consequently sit better in a mix.

Another approach to help fit a reverb tail into the wider context of a mix is equalisation of the reverb tail itself. This allows for the spaciousness of the reverb to be captured without interfering with the frequencies of other elements. Both low frequencies and high frequencies have their pros and cons. In this respect, it's up to the producer to pick whatever they prefer.

The positives and negatives are compared in Figure 4.9:

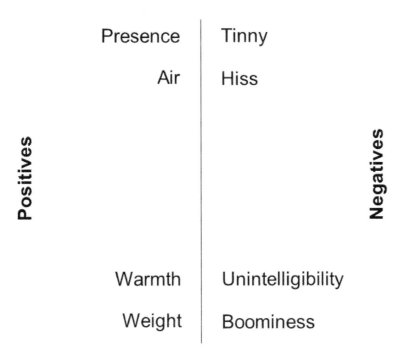

Higher frequencies

Presence	Tinny
Air	Hiss
Warmth	Unintelligibility
Weight	Boominess

Lower frequencies

Figure 4.9: A comparison of the qualities of higher and lower frequency reverb.

Damping mimics the effect of natural rooms, where either lower or higher frequencies will decay more quickly than their opposites, depending on the materials present. Damping is sometimes preferred to equalisation, because it conveys a more natural environment, providing the ear with a realistic psychoacoustic simulation of the space.

High frequency damping simulates rooms with softer, (that is, less reflective) surfaces, where higher frequencies decay faster. Inevitably, the higher the damping, the greater the amount of soft surfaces implied to be present in the room. High frequency damping can also sometimes be used to simulate a large space. Because a bigger space contains more air than a small one, more of the high frequencies will be absorbed. Using a large amount of high frequency damping produces a warmer, more intimate sound, whilst subtle damping creates a more hollow, airy sound.

Bass traps and wood both readily absorb low frequencies. Low frequency damping simulates this process of low-frequency absorption and creates a thinner reverb that can float more easily in a mix, thanks to the absence of low-end 'mud'.

The results of damping are illustrated in Figure 4.10:

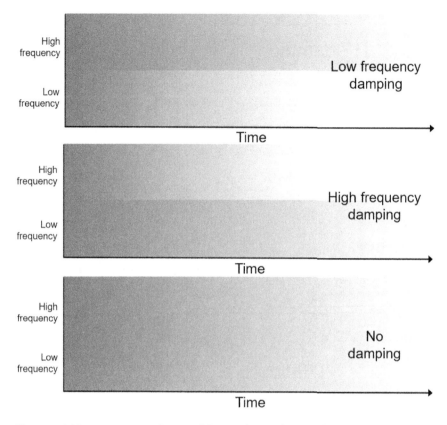

Figure 4.10: A comparison of how damping affects frequencies over time in reverb tails. Low frequency damping means that low frequencies decay faster than higher ones; high frequency damping means that high frequencies decay faster than lower ones.

Depending on the plugin, damping can sometimes be presented as two frequencies—a low and a high. This creates three bands— the low damping band, a middle undamped band and high damping band. This is illustrated in Figure 4.11:

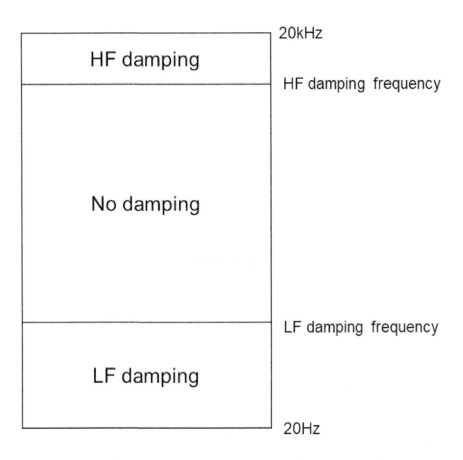

20kHz

HF damping

HF damping frequency

No damping

LF damping frequency

LF damping

20Hz

Figure 4.11: An illustration of damping bands. Notice that the middle band either side of the LF and HF frequencies is unaffected by damping.

Some reverb units use a damping ratio between 0 and 1. This is the ratio between the decay of high frequencies and the decay of low frequencies. When using the ratio option, the damping time will be affected by the decay time you set. A damping ratio of 0.5 over a 2-second decay time for example, will cause the high frequencies to decay within one second—twice as fast as the undamped decay. This is illustrated in Figure 4.12:

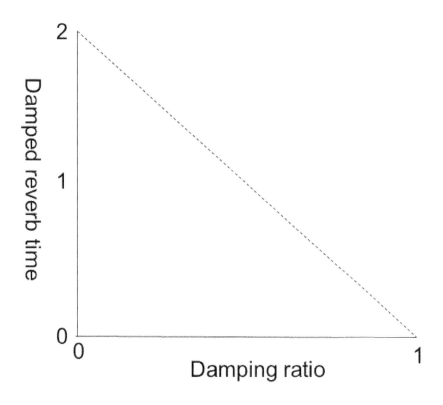

Figure 4.12: An illustration of how the damping ratio affects the damped reverb time of an initial 2-second decay time.

Whether applied to the reverb's input or the reverb tail itself, both damping and equalisation are very good methods by which to slip a reverb tail into a mix. Used discreetly, they can convey a sense of warmth and presence, as well as providing valuable psychoacoustic information about the size of the space and the materials present within it.

4.7: Size & Shape

Size controls the dimensions of a simulated room, from a small vocal booth to a vast arena. Depending upon the volume of the intended space, significant differences will occur both in the early reflections and in the decay time. A smaller sized space means a higher density of reflections will occur, with a faster onset. This translates into a more metallic sound: try clapping your hands in a bathroom or basement to hear an example of this. A larger space leads to a slower attack, greater gaps between the early reflections and a more diffuse, blurred sound, like the effect you'd get from clapping your hands inside an empty community hall.

On reverb devices, size tends to be represented by a numeric value. Historically, this value would represent either the length of a rectangular space in metres, or its total volume expressed in cubic metres. More recently however, the room size will be expressed on a numeric scale with the lowest value representing the smallest possible space and the greatest value the largest, often without indicating the units of measurement involved. A good example of this is Ableton's Reverb, where the Size parameter can be set to any value ranging from 0.22 to 500.

Size is a parameter that needs careful thought. Much depends on the sound you're reverberating. At a bigger size, sounds with slower attacks—such as pads and strings—often glow, but percussion can sound washed out. Conversely, a smaller size is preferable for fast-attacking sounds like percussion, since the faster early reflection densities tie into the transients of the instrument. Pads and strings, meanwhile, can lose luminosity and gain unintended presence in a smaller space.

Some reverb units also offer you the option to control a parameter called Shape. This allows you to select a specific room shape, which of course will alter the behaviour of the early reflections. You can choose from simple shapes that generate fewer early reflections—such as a rectangle or a triangle—to complex asymmetric shapes that create a denser sound.

Shape can also be a linear control (for example from 0 to 100), and in these instances it will set the overlap between early reflections and the reverb tail itself. A low setting here would resemble a simple shape and can create a sharp, direct reverberation, as compared with a high setting, which would represent a complex shape and produce a reverb tail that is less distinct overall.

4.8: Stereo

Stereo is a parameter that controls the stereo width of the reverb. At its lowest setting, it provides a mono reverb tail, whilst at its maximum setting, it creates two independent reverberations that slightly differ in character and are panned to the left and right, creating true stereo width.

Because we have two ears, our perception of reverberations in actual rooms is almost always in stereo, so stereo should usually be maximised for aural authenticity.

Mono reverb has its uses, however. Individual sounds may be panned to the left or to the right of the stereo image, without confusing reflections coming from the opposite side of the stereo field. This proves useful when applying reverb to percussion sounds, such as a shaker being played from a particular position on a stage, for example.

4.9: Modulation

Modulation is often available for application for the reverb tail itself.

Modulation adds a small degree of randomisation to the time between the individual echoes, and this applies constructive and destructive interference to the echo waveforms. An echo in a real-life environment will always be subject to minor fluctuations, such as when travelling through areas of warm and cold air, or because of the differences between reflective and absorptive surfaces. Such variations would be computationally too complex to simulate with any precision, so applying a small amount of modulation to a reverb tail can add realism.

Modulation is normally added through an LFO (low frequency oscillator). It has two controls: *rate* and *amount*. A lower rate means that the randomisation is cycled through more slowly. This will be heard as shifting modulation across a long reverb tail. A higher rate meanwhile will cycle through the randomisation more rapidly, which at its most extreme can add some destructive 'grit' to the reverb tail. This is because the increased speed of the modulation destroys some of the intelligibility of the sound.

Amount, also termed depth, means the extent of the modulation, and works in the same way as a Dry/Wet control. This is illustrated in Figure 4.13:

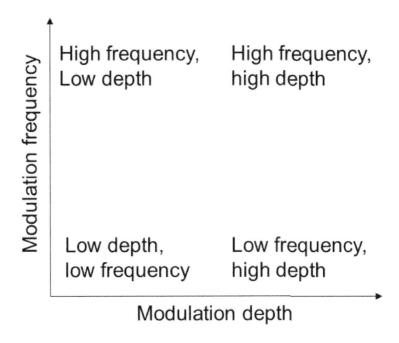

Figure 4.13: An illustration of the two main parameters of modulation: depth and frequency.

Whilst excessive modulation detracts from the realism of the reverb, this can also be viewed as helpful; some of the most exciting reverb results are arrived at directly through the creation of unrealistic spaces.

4.10: Specific algorithms

When working with digital reverb, it's important to distinguish between a *preset*, and an *algorithm*.

As you'll discover, some reverb devices, such as Ableton's Reverb, provide you with a set of parameters, and *all* presets are some variation of these parameters. Other reverb devices meanwhile, such as ValhallaRoom, will offer you a set of algorithms. These are distinct computational templates, and the parameters of the device tweak this template.

This is an important distinction to understand, because a lot of the character of the reverb comes from the algorithm. Whereas devices based upon a single algorithm (with different presets) will have a particular character, devices with lots of different algorithms have several types of character, depending upon the algorithm chosen.

When exploring reverb presets or algorithms, you'll often encounter common terms such as Room, Hall, Chamber, etc.

Whilst these terms are now largely anachronistic, they can act as a useful frame of reference when discussing reverbs:

- *Room* reverbs usually have prominent early reflections and a shorter decay. They are useful for enlivening drums, vocals, or acoustic instruments. When used delicately they can maintain a sense of intimacy. They sound fairly dry because of a lower decay time.

- *Hall* reverbs should simulate concert halls, with slower early reflections, a longer reverb time and a fairly even frequency distribution. They can slightly blur the sound, creating the overlaps between notes and reverb tails that could be expected in a real concert hall. They do require judicious handling however; over-use of hall reverb can make a mix sound mushy. Hall reverbs are often used for orchestral music, choral vocals, or pads.

- *Chamber* reverbs should simulate the reverb chambers and/or echo rooms built into music studios, as mentioned in Section 4.2. They produce dense reverb tails with a fast attack, but fewer early reflections. The ambience of their quirky frequency responses can sound great on recordings. They are a useful all-rounder reverb and are designed for clarity.

- *Spring*—as its name implies—simulates the artificial reverbs discussed in Section 4.2: Spring Reverb and possesses a prominent twanging sound. Spring is of little use for simulating actual reverberation, but its distinctive behaviour can sound fantastic on individual percussive hits or synthesizer stabs. It is one of the cornerstone effects of the Dub sound.

- *Plate* simulates the artificial reverb plates discussed in Section 4.3: Plate Reverb. They have a bright attack and a warm, dark decay, with the higher frequencies decaying before the lower ones. When pushed, they can create a distinctive twang. Because in the original reverb device the physical plates are a two-dimensional sheet, the reflection density in this algorithm or preset stays the same throughout the reverb. This intimate sound can work wonders on elements that need to be warmed up.

Table 4.1 summarizes the above reverb types, including the reverbs most typically used for particular instruments:

Table 4.1: A summary of the main reverb types.

Reverb type	Early reflections	Reverb tail	Character	Often used for
Room	Prominent	Fast	Intimate, lively	Drums, acoustic instruments, vocals
Hall	Fairly prominent	Slow	Grandiose	Orchestral music, choral vocals, pads
Chamber	Not very prominent	Medium	Strong, quirky	All-rounder
Spring	None	Fast	Distinctive	Percussive hits
Plate	Minimal	Variable	Warm	All-rounder

In this Chapter, we've looked at the most common basic parameters to be found across reverb devices. Equipped with this information, you are now in a suitable position to move fairly seamlessly between different reverb plugins.

If you would like to hear examples of all five of the algorithms presented in this section, you can download the sound of a guitar being played through each one of them from:

https://reverb.producers.guide.

Chapter 5: Individual Reverb Units

Having looked at the basic parameters of reverb devices, we'll now focus on the practical use of four well-known, widely used individual reverb plugins, examining them in some detail. This will enable you to understand not only their individual functions, but the commonalities and differences between them.

To help you gain knowledge that will be directly transferrable to any reverb device you encounter in the future, I've chosen four reverb devices that each work in different ways:

- Ableton's stock reverb unit. This will familiarise you with one of the most used stock reverb units.

- Valhalla DSP's ValhallaRoom. This is a budget option known for outstanding results. It will also give you a feel for how contemporary plugin designers are taking reverb to the next level.

- Logic's ChromaVerb. This will provide insight into one of the more unusual methods of reverberation available on the market.

- Logic's Space Designer. This will help you learn how to use convolution reverb.

Let's begin with a dissection of Ableton's stock reverb.

5.1: Ableton's stock reverb

The first thing to note about Ableton's stock reverb is its layout.
Moving from left to right, it reflects the natural order of a workflow.
On the left therefore, you will see the controls for input processing.
To the right of this lies a control for managing the early reflections,
whilst the rest of the plugin is for control of the reverb tail itself.

The whole plugin is depicted in Figure 5.1:

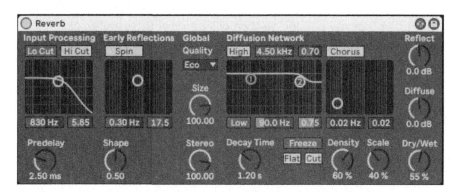

Figure 5.1: Ableton's stock reverb plugin.

The functions of this plugin can effectively be divided into four
sections, as shown in Figure 5.2:

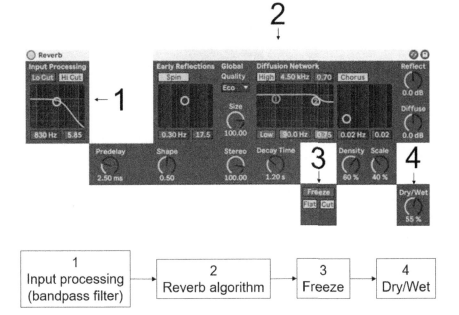

Figure 5.2: The four sections of Ableton's stock reverb plugin.

All the *Input Processing* parameters control a simple band-pass filter. The Freeze section governs the *Freeze* function (which we'll get to later in this Section) and the *Dry/Wet* parameter controls the balance between the reverberated and unreverberated signals.

We'll begin by working through Ableton's reverb unit from left to right, starting with *Input Processing*, as shown in Figure 5.3:

Figure 5.3: The Input Processing area of Ableton's Reverb.

Input Processing is the point at which you can filter the audio signal before it arrives at the reverb algorithm. It restricts the frequencies that you allow into the reverb. You may wish to remove the lower frequencies of a bass guitar for example, to prevent them from being reverberated and creating a muddy texture.

You can use the Lo Cut and Hi Cut buttons at the top to choose which type of filter to use. Table 5.1 shows a comparison of these filters:

Table 5.1: The buttons of the Input Processing area compared with their resulting filter types.

Button activated	Filter type
Lo Cut	Highpass
Hi Cut	Lowpass
Both	Bandpass
Neither	Allpass (none)

The two horizontal sliders along the bottom, as seen in Figure 5.3, allow you to select the filter frequency and its bandwidth. A low bandwidth means a narrow filter, and a high bandwidth means a wide filter.

The next control is *Predelay*, which controls the amount of delay prior to the early reflections, as shown in Figure 5.4:

Figure 5.4: The Predelay pot on Ableton's Reverb.

Predelay allows you to select a range that extends from 1ms to 250ms, covering all needs of creative sound design, from the conventional to the advanced. The natural range of predelay stretches from 1ms to around 25ms. For more unusual effects, something between 50ms to 250ms will be required.

The next control is *Early Reflections*, as shown in Figure 5.5:

Figure 5.5: The Early Reflections section of Ableton's Reverb.

By using the *Spin* button, you can apply modulation to the reverb's early reflections. The XY pad allows you to select the LFO frequency and amplitude of this modulation, although you can also use the two slides underneath the pad. You can choose the duration of a modulation cycle with the frequency parameter, whilst the amplitude parameter lets you decide the extent of the modulation to be applied. This adds some natural randomness to your early reflections. Be aware however that too much modulation can lend an artificial feel to your sound.

Underneath *Spin* is the *Shape* dial, which allows you to choose the prominence of the early reflections, as well as their overlap with the reverb tail itself. A low *Shape* makes the early reflections decay more gradually, often overlapping with the reverb tail to create the impression of a more complex space, whereas a high *Shape* makes the early reflections decay quickly, implying a simpler one.

Next, we have the *Global* section. This is where you will choose the parameters that affect the overall reverb tail, as seen in Figure 5.6:

Figure 5.6: The Global section of Ableton's Reverb.

The top parameter contains a drop-down menu that allows you to select from three settings to govern the quality of the reverb simulation:

- *Eco*, which is light on CPU use, but provides the crudest simulation of a reverberated space.

- *High*, which uses much more CPU, but provides the most sophisticated simulation.

- *Medium*, which is a compromise between Eco and High.

It might seem the case to always pick *High* if you have a good processor, but the lower quality offered by *Eco* can give your reverb some added crunch and character, which is sometimes helpful in genres like dub techno.

The middle parameter is *Size*. This enables you to control the size of the virtual room, the smallest setting providing a dense, metallic sound and the highest an open, diffuse sound. The *Size* settings range from 0.22 to 500. This setting seems to be more of an algorithmic variable than the simulation of a real, measured space.

The bottom parameter is *Stereo*, which ranges from 0 to 120. At 0, the reverb is in mono, whilst at 120, two similar but distinct reverb tails will occur, one in the left channel and the other in the right. When using *Stereo*, consider the placement of your instruments on the stereo stage. As discussed in Chapter 4, wide instruments such as large synthetic pads will benefit from a high *Stereo* value, whereas a sound that would be placed at a single point, such as a simple drum hit, will benefit from a low *Stereo* value.

The next section to the right is the *Diffusion Network*, which contains an XY pad filter and an XY pad chorus, as seen in Figure 5.7:

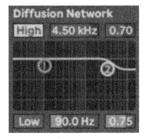

Figure 5.7: The Diffusion Network section of Ableton's Reverb.

Just like the *Input Processing* filter, the *Diffusion Network* filter will provide you with different filter types depending on the buttons selected, as shown in Table 5.2:

Button activated	Filter type
Lo Cut	Highpass
Hi Cut	Lowpass
Both	Bandpass
Neither	Allpass (none)

It's important to note the difference between the *Diffusion Network* filter and the *Input Processing* filter we looked at earlier. Whereas the *Input Processing* filter filters the sound coming into the reverb, the *Diffusion Network* filter applies the filter over the course of the reverb tail. This changes how frequencies will decay over time, making its effects more complex. It is this functionality that enables you to create more realistic simulations by letting some frequencies decay faster than others.

Chorus allows you to add additional chorus modulation. When activated by selecting the *Chorus* button, the XY pad enables you to change both the frequency and extent of the modulation. Just like *Early Reflections* modulation, *Chorus* lets you add some natural randomness to the reverb tail.

Below the *Diffusion Network* filter and the *Chorus* section are four further important parameters: *Decay Time, Freeze, Density* and *Scale,* as shown in Figure 5.8:

Figure 5.8: The Decay Time, Freeze, Density and Scale parameters.

Decay Time allows you to set the RT60 of the reverb tail, from the minimal 200ms to an extreme 60 seconds. Even though *Decay Time* is a single parameter, it is one of the most essential and you will spend a lot of enjoyable time adjusting it!

When the *Freeze* section is activated by clicking the *Freeze* button, the reverb tail will be frozen in place (it will stay lit when active). This means that the sound reverberates continuously and doesn't decay, allowing you to hear the character of the reverberation in isolation. You won't have to trigger your sounds repeatedly, trying to hear the reverb tail before it decays.

To further assist you in reviewing your reverb tail, you can also enable *Flat* to bypass any filtering placed on the frozen signal by the reverb algorithm. After *Freeze* has been activated, *Cut* will prevent any further sounds from contributing to the frozen sound, which is helpful when you want to isolate the reverberation of one part of your track.

Density controls the how dense the reverb tail is by changing how closely the echoes are packed together. This extends from 0.1%, which makes the reverb tail thin, to 96%, which makes the reverb tail thick.

The *Scale* parameter controls the frequency response of the reverb tail, with a higher value corresponding to a darker tail (one with less high frequency content) and a lower value keeping more sparkle.

The final three parameters to the right are arguably the most important of all. These are the *Reflect*, *Diffuse* and *Dry/Wet* controls, as shown in Figure 5.9:

Figure 5.9: The Reflect, Diffuse and Dry/Wet parameters.

Reflect and *Diffuse* allow you to control the amplitude of the early reflections and reverb tail, respectively. This will assist you to not only control the reverb but to listen to each component of the overall reverb tail in isolation.

Below *Reflect* and *Diffuse* you will see the *Dry/Wet* mixer. This enables you to select between the original sound source and the reverb tail. If you're attempting to get to grips with Ableton's reverb for the first time, I recommend setting the reverb to 100% Wet and isolating either the early reflections or the later reverb tail. You can do this by cutting the volume of one or other of the parameters. To hear the early reflections alone, reduce the volume of *Diffuse*. To hear the reverb tail alone, reduce the volume of *Reflect*. In this way you can monitor each dimension of the reverb tail.

What's interesting about Ableton's reverb is that unlike many digital reverbs, it doesn't use separate algorithms for different scenarios; instead, it attempts to cater for every conceivable type of reverb with its presets alone.

Figure 5.10 for example, depicts the *Main Hall* preset:

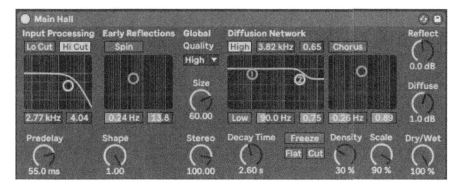

Figure 5.10: The Main Hall preset on Ableton Live's Reverb.

You can immediately observe:

- A substantial *Predelay*.

- A wide stereo image, using the *Stereo* parameter.

- A 2.6 second RT60, using the *Decay Time* parameter.

- The faster decay of higher frequencies within the *Diffusion Network*.

- A lack of modulation in both the *Spin* and the *Chorus* sections.

- A darker reverb tail (using the *Scale* control).

- A slight emphasis on the latter part of the reverb tail (*Diffuse* is 1dB higher than *Reflect*).

Now compare the *Main Hall* preset shown in Figure 5.10 above, with the *Small Chamber* preset in Figure 5.11 below:

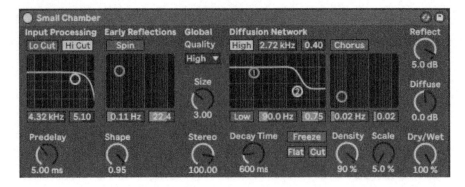

Figure 5.11: The Small Chamber preset on Ableton Live's Reverb.

- The *Input Processing* low-pass filter has a higher cutoff point.

- It has a short 5ms *Predelay*.

- It has a tiny *Size* setting.

- The RT60, controlled by the *Decay Time* parameter is only 600ms.

- Its higher frequencies delay quickly within the *Diffusion Network*.

- It has a large emphasis on early reflections, with *Reflect* 5dB higher than *Diffuse*.

The industry standard stock reverb presets provided by Ableton's engineers offer a great opportunity to study the basic attributes of the most well-known reverb types.

Ableton's stock reverb is a workhorse, capable of a simulating diverse range of reverberated environments. There are however many ways to simulate reverberation and in the next section we'll examine another method, that provided by Valhalla DSP's ValhallaRoom.

5.2: ValhallaRoom

The superb ValhallaRoom reverb unit is created by reverb specialists Valhalla DSP and described by them as *'An Algorithmic Vision Of Perfection And Precision. It's Grade A Class, Number One In Its Division'*.

Hyperbole aside, ValhallaRoom is a great plugin for anyone wanting to explore an alternative to the stock plugins that came with their DAW. It can offer a more well-rounded sound than Ableton's stock reverb and is reasonably priced.

At first glance, ValhallaRoom's interface is simpler than Ableton's, with 5 global parameters to the left, then 6 or 8 parameters on the right, that control the early or late reflections, as shown in Figure 5.12:

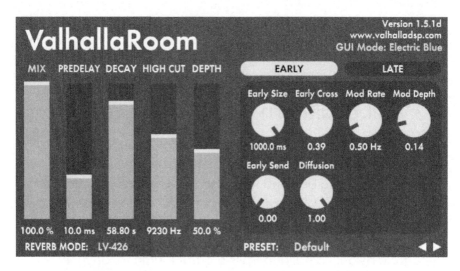

Figure 5.12: Valhalla DSP's ValhallaRoom.

At the top-right, you will see *EARLY* and *LATE*.

If you select *EARLY*, the dials below these selectors will allow you to edit the early reflection parameters, as shown in Figure 5.12, above. If you select *LATE*, these dials will now alter to allow you to edit the reverb tail parameters, as shown in Figure 5.13, below:

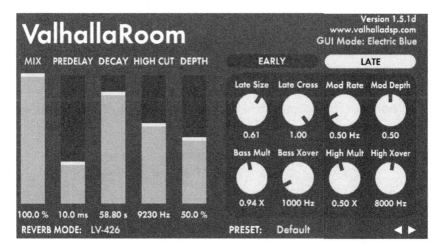

Figure 5.13: The Late parameters on Valhalla DSP's ValhallaRoom.

On the left, you can see the five global parameters that represent the heart of this reverb device. These parameters are global because they affect the entire reverb tail, from its early reflections through to its final decay. These parameters may be familiar by now:

- *Mix* governs how much of the original signal and how much of the reverberated signal is output, just like *Dry/Wet* in Ableton.

- *Predelay* controls the extent to which the reverberated sound is initially delayed.

- *Decay* is the RT60 of the reverb tail.

- *High Cut* is the cutoff of a low-pass filter applied to the input signal.

- *Depth* controls the balance between the *Early Reflections* and *Late* reverb tail sections. At 0% *Depth* you will hear the

EARLY section only. At 100% *Depth* you will hear the *LATE* section only. All values between 0%—100% will therefore result in a proportional mix between the two.

As you can see from Figure 5.14, ValhallaRoom's controls over the early reflections are like those offered by Ableton's stock reverb:

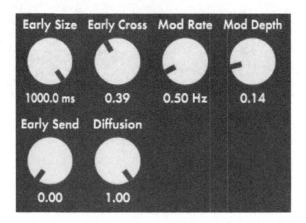

Figure 5.14: Six parameters on ValhallaRoom.

The basic descriptions for each parameter on ValhallaRoom's interface become available when you hover your mouse over them, however I am providing some additional information here, to help you relate ValhallaRoom to what you've learned about Ableton's *Reverb*:

- *Early Size* controls both the size of early reflections, and the attack time of the reverb. The lower the *Early Size* value, the smaller the early reflections and the faster the attack of the reverb. Higher settings result in a nonlinear or gated reverb decay, so the early reflections cut off more abruptly.

- *Early Cross* controls the stereo image of the early reflections. At a lower value, the left and right channels operate fairly independently of one another. A higher value means that they feed into one another, so that the early reflections bounce between the left and right channels.

- *Mod Rate* controls the frequency of the early reverb modulation, just like the *Spin* function on Ableton's stock reverb.

- *Mod Depth* controls the extent of the early reverb modulation, from 0 for no modulation at all, to 1.00 for the maximum modulation possible.

- *Early Send* controls the how much of the early reflections are sent to the input of the late reverb. A higher value creates a more continuous reverb tail, as the early reflections are fed into the feedback networks of the reverb tail.

- *Diffusion* controls the density of the early reflections, ranging from 0 for the lowest possible density to 1.00 for the maximum.

Figure 5.15 below shows the parameters of the LATE section:

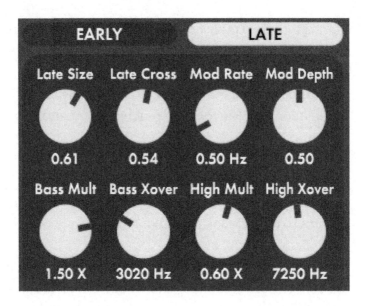

Figure 5.15: The Late section of ValhallaRoom.

- *Late Size* controls the theoretical room size, and *Late Cross* the stereo spread.

- *Mod Rate* and *Mod Depth* control the modulation of the late reverb tail, with *Mod Rate* determining the speed of the modulation and *Mod Depth* determining modulation.

- *Bass Mult* and *High Mult* scale the decay time for low and high frequencies. This means the global *Decay* parameter can be multiplied by the *Bass Mult* and *High Mult* parameters (which operate independently of one another) to decide what decay time you'd like on the low, middle, and high frequencies.

- *Bass Xover* and *High Xover* control the crossover frequencies— the points where the *Bass Mult* and *High Xover* frequencies kick in. In Figure 5.15 above, for example, frequencies under 3020Hz would be multiplied by 1.5 and frequencies above 7250Hz multiplied by 0.6, creating a reverb with a longer bass decay.

As you can see, the functionalities of ValhallaRoom and Ableton Live's Reverb unit are similar. They are both outstanding devices, but in my opinion ValhallaRoom has the edge, for its characterful, warm sound. Ableton Live's Reverb does a respectable job of basic reverb, for when you don't wish to add any character to your reverberations.

The most important way in which ValhallaRoom differs from Ableton's stock Reverb however, is the sheer variety of algorithms on offer. Ableton's presets all possess a similar character. ValhallaRoom's has several algorithms, each one honed, as shown in Figure 5.16:

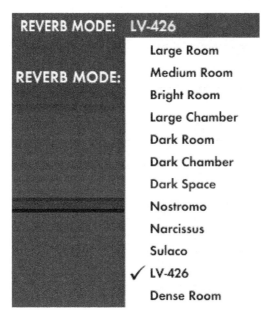

Figure 5.16: The different algorithms available in ValhallaRoom.

For example, it describes LV-426 as *"downsampled, very slow reverb attack, lush random modulation, dark tone".* (All

ValhallaRoom reverb algorithms come with vivid descriptions like this.)

It is important to understand that these are *not* presets—they are algorithms. Even if your parameters stay the same, changing the algorithm will give your reverb a completely new character. To get a genuine sense of this, you will need to spend some time exploring these algorithms. There is a free demo of ValhallaRoom available at www.valhalladsp.com if you want to experiment.

Next, we will look at a new and quite different approach to programming reverb: Logic Pro X's ChromaVerb.

5.3: ChromaVerb

Just like Ableton's reverb, Logic Pro X's ChromaVerb is an all-purpose reverb device, but one distinguished by its novel workflow.

Look at Figure 5.17. Unlike other reverbs, the first thing that you'll notice is that the display is dominated by an equaliser. It's this function that we'll delve into first:

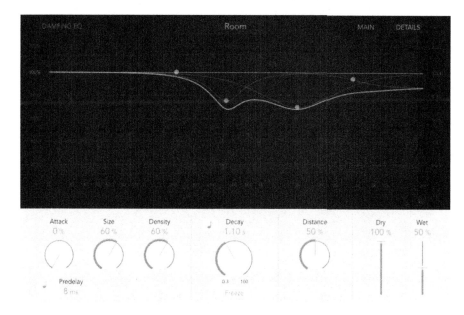

Figure 5.17: Logic Pro X's ChromaVerb.

The equaliser allows you to change the RT60 for each frequency, thus shaping the frequency response of the space. The frequency responses range from 0% to 200% (i.e., zero to double) the Decay time selected.

Figure 5.18 shows a simplified view of the ChromaVerb interface based on a *Decay* of 2 seconds:

Figure 5.18: A simplified view of ChromaVerb's equaliser.

Changing the *Decay* time pot on the front panel alters the decay times; the percentages available remain the same, but the numbers will change. In Figure 5.19 below, for example, I've changed the *Decay* time to 800ms. Note how the figures to the right of the view have adjusted:

Figure 5.19: Note that the times on the equaliser have adjusted in response to the different RT60.

One virtue of ChromaVerb is that you can move the nodes on the reverb's equaliser, in a manner like a standard EQ. These nodes allow you to alter the RT60 of individual frequencies within the simulated space with high precision. This is like the Damping function but applied with a far greater level of accuracy. In Figure 5.20, for example, the RT60 of frequencies above 4k will decay around 75ms faster than the RT60 of those below 4k:

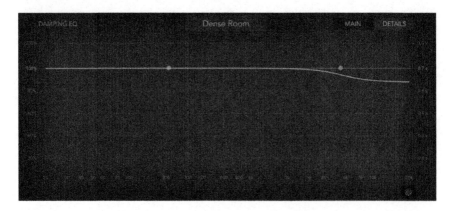

Figure 5.20: ChromaVerb's equaliser.

If you are using a newer Mac, you can also visualise your reverb's

decay by clicking on the small button in the bottom-right: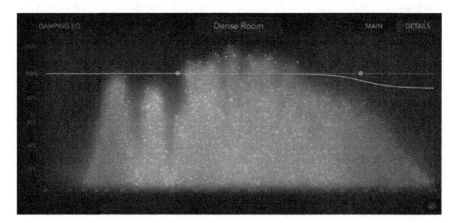
to generate the display shown in Figure 5.21:

Figure 5.21: The rather beautiful visualisation in ChromaVerb.

This visualisation can be helpful for viewing the decay times of the frequencies of your reverb.

One of the most important functions of ChromaVerb is the algorithm selector, shown in Figure 5.22: which becomes available by clicking above the centre of the EQ view.

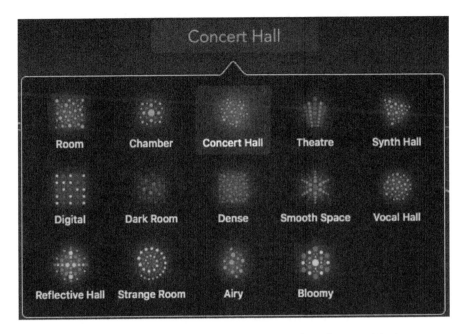

Figure 5.22: The algorithm selector in ChromaVerb.

To change an algorithm, you click its icon. Selecting different algorithms will not change the underlying parameters, however; these algorithms merely alter how the selected algorithm processes the reverb.

The controllers for these parameters are split into two tabs: *MAIN* and *DETAILS*.

Let's begin by looking at the parameters within the *MAIN* tab, shown in Figure 5.23:

Figure 5.23: *The parameters within ChromaVerb's Main tab.*

Moving from left to right:

- *Attack* affects either the volume or the density build-up time, depending on the chosen room type:

    - In room types *Theatre, Dense Room, Smooth Space, Reflective Hall, Strange Room* and *Airy,* the *Attack* parameter increases volume over time.

    - In room types *Room, Chamber, Concert Hall, Synth Hall, Digital, Dark Room, Vocal Hall* and *Bloomy,* the *Attack* parameter sets the time it takes for the reverb to reach the maximum density value as determined by the *Density* parameter.

- *Size* configures the dimensions of the room. Higher values correspond to a larger space.

- *Density* simultaneously changes the density of both the early and late reflections, depending on the room type.

- *Predelay* sets the time between the start of the original signal and the early reflections.

- *Predelay Sync* sets predelay values to divisions automatically synchronised with the track tempo. It is activated by pressing the eighth-note button next to *Predelay.*

Within the second area, in the middle:

- *Decay* sets the decay time—the RT60—which is frequency dependent, according to the configuration of the main equaliser above these parameters.

- *Decay Sync* configures decay values to divisions synchronised with the track tempo. It is activated by pressing the eighth-note button next to *Decay.*

- *Freeze* holds the reverb signal infinitely, so that it can be previewed in depth (just like the *Freeze* function in Ableton Live's Reverb).

Within the final two sections on the right:

- *Distance* adjusts the perceived distance from the source by altering early and late energy. An emphasis on early reflections generally implies closeness to the source, whereas an emphasis on late reflections implies distance.

- *Dry/Wet* mixes the amount of 'dry', non-reverberated signal with the chosen amount of 'wet' or reverberated signal.

Now let's explore the *Details* tab of ChromaVerb. Here you will find parameters for a more nuanced control of your reverberation. You'll have probably already noticed broad similarities between these algorithmic reverb devices

and can probably predict the function of most of the parameters that follow, shown below in Figure 5.24:

Figure 5.24: The Details tab of ChromaVerb.

- *Quality* allows you to choose a quality level, much like Ableton's Reverb unit. *Low* produces a crunchy, CPU-efficient reverb. *High* offers an acceptable balance between CPU use and quality. *Ultra* will give you the highest possible quality reverb, albeit at the expense of CPU.

- *Mod Speed*, *Mod Depth* and *Mod Source* control the speed, amount, and shape of added modulation.

- *Smoothing* alters the shape of the LFO waveform. It smooths the Random LFO and saturates the sine and noise waveforms, so that you can add more modulation via the *Mod Depth* parameter without creating jarring artefacts.

- *Early/Late Mix* sets the balance between the early and late reflections, which depends on the *Distance* parameter you've set. This is because the *Distance* parameter also sets the balance between early and late reflections. The difference in this case, is that *Early/Late Mix* is a basic mixer, whereas *Distance* uses the reverb's algorithm, meaning that changes you make using *Distance* will vary the fundamental character of the reverberation. To achieve the results you want, you may therefore need to iteratively balance this parameter with the *Distance* parameter.

- *Width* controls the stereo width of the reverb.

- *Mono maker* sets a minimum frequency threshold for stereo imaging, so that you can remove low-frequency stereo information. This is helpful when reverberating tracks with low-frequency content, since stereo low-frequency reverb can add mud to your mix, and cause issues if you plan on pressing your tracks to vinyl. You may even wish to filter these low frequencies out entirely before they enter your reverb.

- The last feature to mention on ChromaVerb is the *Output EQ*, which allows you to sculpt the output equalisation of the reverb tail in detail. This EQ is shown in Figure 5.25:

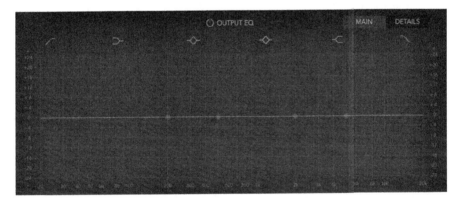

Figure 5.25: ChromaVerb's Output EQ.

This sculpting can be done in the same manner that you would use a parametric equaliser, with different filter types enabling you to achieve the shape that you want.

As you will have observed in this Section, whilst algorithmic reverb plugins differ in the terms used for their functions, they nonetheless possess many features in common. For ease of reference, Table 5.3 below compares the three reverb units we've looked at so far in this Chapter:

Table 5.3: A comparison of the features of Ableton's Reverb, ValhallaRoom and ChromaVerb.

Feature	Ableton Reverb	ValhallaRoom	Chromaverb
Input EQ	✔ (Input Processing)	✔ (High Cut)	✖
Predelay	✔ (Predelay)	✔ (Predelay)	✔ (Predelay)
Early reflections only modulation	✔ (Spin)	✔ (Mod Rate & Mod Depth)	✖
Build-up time	✖	✖	✔ (Attack)
Early reflection/reverb tail overlap	✔ (Shape)	✔ (Early Send)	✔ (Distance)
Early reflection/reverb tail balance	✔ (Reflect and Diffuse)	✔ (Depth)	✔ (Early/Late)
Size	✔ (Size)	✖ (Although different algorithms have different implied sizes)	✔ (Size)
Early reflection stereo width	✖	✔ (Early Cross)	✔ (Width)
Reverb tail stereo width	✔ (Stereo)	✔ (Late Cross)	✔ (Width)
Stereo width cutoff	✖	✖	✔ (Mono Mix)
Reverb tail EQ	✔ (Diffusion Network)	✔ (Bass and High Mult and Xover)	✔ (Damping EQ)
Decay time (RT60)	✔ (Decay Time)	✔ (Decay)	✔ (Decay)
Reverb tail modulation	✔ (Chorus)	✔ (Mod Rate & Depth)	✔ (Mod Speed & Depth)
Density	✔ (Density)	✔ (Diffusion)	✔ (Density)
Quality	✔ (Quality)	✖	✔ (Quality)
Algorithm choice	✖	✔ (Reverb Mode)	✔
Wet/Dry	✔ (Dry/Wet)	✔ (Mix)	✔ (Dry/Wet)

You will see from this table that the way each parameter affects the overall sound will largely depend upon the plugin used, the algorithm it employs, and its interpretation of common controls. Most reverb plugins have enough in common however to enable you to move between them without encountering too many problems.

Because the individual implementation of reverb algorithms can differ so much between units, it's worth spending time getting to know each of your own reverb plugins in some depth, to avoid confusion. The balance between early reflections and the reverb tail, for example, can be controlled in all three of the plugins we've considered, but is called *Reflect/Diffuse*, *Depth* or *Early/Late*, depending on which plugin you're using.

We'll complete this Chapter by looking at the other major form of artificial reverb: convolution. The plugin we'll be using for this is Logic's Space Designer.

5.4: Space Designer

As previously described, convolution reverb works differently to algorithmic reverb. It takes a captured impulse response from an established space and 'convolves' it with the incoming sound signal. It then adds a reverb tail that mimics the reverb tail of the original impulse response, resulting in a sound that now behaves as though it was being played within the captured space.

Impulse response files are not a special format. Comprising recorded noise in .wav format, they can be played alone and often sound like a reverberated white noise pulse or a reverberated sine wave sweep. Figure 5.26, for example, depicts an impulse response captured in a New York underpass:

Figure 5.26: An impulse response captured in a New York underpass.

When you open Space Designer and first load a patch, the most prominent part you'll see is the waveform and envelope, as shown in Figure 5.27:

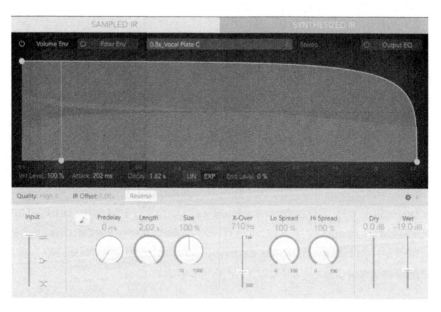

Figure 5.27: Space Designer's waveform and envelope.

The large, curved shape in the foreground is the envelope, which allows you to change the intensity of the impulse response across the Decay time. In the background is the impulse response itself.

Space Designer's controls are more limited than those that would be expected on an algorithmic reverb, and with good reason; the largest variances in reverb character come from the impulse responses themselves, rather than the parameters of the device. Given the vast number of impulse responses packaged with Space Designer, your focus will be the selection of the most suitable one for your sound. You can, however, make use of Space Designer's parameters to stretch or fine-tune your reverb tail.

Space Designer offers two methods for harnessing impulse responses: you can choose a sampled impulse response, or a synthesized impulse response that you create yourself. These are selectable using the top bar, as shown in Figure 5.28:

SAMPLED IR   SYNTHESIZED IR

Figure 5.28: The Impulse Response selector, offering SAMPLED IR or SYNTHESIZED IR.

Let's explore the sampled impulse responses (*SAMPLED IR*) first. These can be loaded by clicking on the central selector above the waveform and selecting *Load IR*, as shown in Figure 5.29:

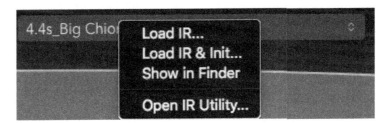

Figure 5.29: The Load IR function in Space Designer.

Load IR brings up Finder, which displays a directory structure containing a substantial number of impulse responses, such as those shown in Figure 5.30:

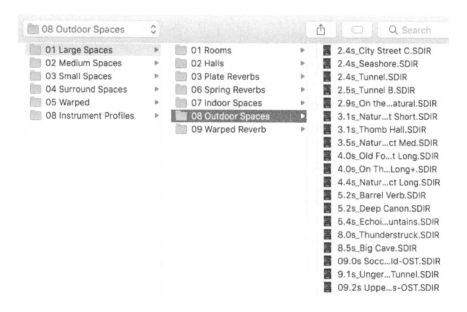

Figure 5.30: The abundance of impulse responses.

Clicking an impulse response automatically loads it. If you choose *Load IR & Init*, the plugin's parameters will also revert to a basic default and set your *Decay* length to that of the impulse response.

Once loaded, there are two parameters available to shape the impulse response: *Volume Env* and *Filter Env*, as shown in Figure 5.31. They can be found along the top:

Figure 5.31: The two types of envelopes available in Space Designer.

The first one, *Volume Env*, allows you to add further shape to the amplitude of the impulse response over time. It does so through an Attack and Decay envelope, which itself has four controls:

- *Init Level* sets the initial level of the envelope.

- *Attack* sets the time it takes for the envelope to reach its maximum volume from the level set by *Init Level*. (If *Init Level* is set at 100%, changing *Attack* will have no effect, because the volume cannot increase beyond the level of 100%.)

- *Decay* sets the time it takes for the impulse response to end.

- *End Level* sets the ending level of the envelope. If *End Level* is less than 100%, an early *Decay* time can mean an abrupt end to the impulse response, however this will be less noticeable if it occurs late in the tail, when volume levels are already very low.

- *LIN/EXP* allows you to set whether the curves applied by your envelope are linear (in a straight line) or exponential (curved). A linear envelope means the intensity of the envelope drops consistently over time in a smooth gradient, whereas a curved envelope means it drops suddenly, then gradually diminishes in intensity.

You'll notice that when you make changes, Space Designer takes a moment to apply them, after which they'll become visibly reflected in the waveform. This is because convolution reverbs must redo the convolution process whenever changes are made to the impulse response.

The other section for shaping the impulse response is *Filter Env*. This parameter allows you to add a sweeping filter to your impulse response, changing the frequency response of your reverb tail over time. The *Filter Env* function is shown below in Figure 5.32:

Figure 5.32: The Filter Envelope function on Space Designer.

You can set the filter in the lower-right area of this view. It provides the following options:

- 6dB low-pass: a mild low-pass filter.

- 12dB low-pass: a low-pass filter that will temper the top end of the reverb tail.

- 6dB band-pass: a band-pass filter that will keep a wide range of frequencies around the band selected.

- 12dB high-pass: a high-pass filter that will temper the bottom end of the reverb tail.

The envelope works in the same way as the volume envelope, but instead of modifying the volume over time, you change the filter over time:

- *Init Freq* sets the initial cutoff frequency.

- *Attack* sets the time to reach the *Break Level*.

- *Break Level* sets the maximum cutoff frequency reached by the filter. Once it reaches the *Break Level*, the filter moves to the *Decay* phase.

- *Decay* sets the time to reach the frequency defined by *End Freq*.

- *End Freq* sets the final filter frequency.

Once Space Designer has loaded the modified impulse response, the waveform's appearance will change in response. Compared to Figure 5.32, you will notice that the waveform changes in response to the abrupt change in Filter Env in Figure 5.33:

Figure 5.33: The waveform of the impulse response changes in response to an adjustment in the filter envelope.

Beneath the impulse response on Space Designer, you will find parameters for shaping the reverb tail further. These are presented across four sections, as shown in Figure 5.34:

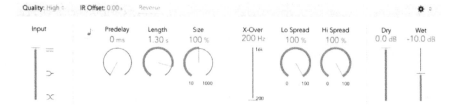

Figure 5.34: Shaping parameters within Space Designer.

Let's look at these in a little more detail from left to right, beginning with the *Quality* section. This provides you with four drop-down options:

- *Lo-Fi* is a grainy interpretation of the impulse response.

- *Low* is a less grainy, but efficient processing of the impulse response.

- *Medium* offers a suitable compromise between CPU efficiency and quality.

- *High* provides the highest quality reverb tail.

Below *Quality* is an *Input* selector that allows you to change the stereo image of the impulse response, as shown in Figure 5.35:

Quality: High

Input

Figure 5.35: The quality and input selector on Space Designer.

Below *Quality* is an *Input* selector that allows you to change the stereo image of the impulse response. You can select between three stereo options, as illustrated by the glyphs:

- Top: the stereo image of the impulse response is maintained.

- Centre: the impulse response is converted to mono.

- Bottom: the left and right channels are swapped over.

The next section is *IR Offset*, which governs the timing of the reverb tail, shown in Figure 5.36:

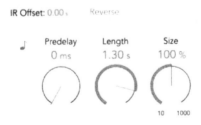

Figure 5.36: The timing settings on Space Designer.

- *IR Offset* allows you to shift the starting point of the impulse response. Changing the offset of a 1834ms impulse response to 1000ms for example, reduces the maximum available length to 834ms by cutting off the first second, as seen in Figure 5.37:

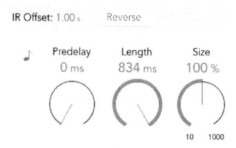

Figure 5.37: Notice the change of maximum length in response to the change of offset.

- The *Reverse* button lets you reverse the impulse response. This can be a way to create artificial 'builds' in the sound, a technique we'll look at in more detail in Chapter 7.

- *Predelay* allows you to set a certain delay period before the reverb tail starts, by physically adding a silence to the start of the convolution process. This can be helpful for more artificial effects, or a subtle reverb on a vocal where you want to make sure that the vocalist's words remain 'dry' and intelligible.

- *Length* and *Size* work with one another. When changing either parameter, the scale of the waveform within the display will change. *Length* alters the length of the impulse response, time, expanding or contracting its duration, much like the *Decay Time* parameter on algorithmic reverbs. There is a minor loss of quality when altering *Length*, but if the change is small, it shouldn't be noticeable. If drastic changes to the length of a convolution reverb are required, you may find it easier to select a different impulse response altogether. *Size*, meanwhile, changes the sample rate of the impulse response, increasing or reducing the perceptual size of the space.

The overall impulse response length equals the *Length* multiplied by the *Size*. This means that a 5 second *Length* impulse response at 20% *Size* will transform the impulse response to 1 second long. In similar vein, a 3 second *Length* impulse response at 1000% *Size* would create a 30 second impulse response.'

The next section governs stereo spread.

- To the right of *X-Over* you will see two sections, *Lo Spread* and *Hi Spread*. These work as percentages up to 100%. Unlike algorithmic reverb, convolution reverb uses impulse responses that already have stereo image information recorded. This means that further stereo information cannot be added. Which frequencies are affected by *Lo Spread* and which are affected by *Hi Spread* is chosen via the *X-Over* frequency. This is helpful when you require certain frequency sections—such as lower frequencies for example—to have less stereo information. This section is depicted in Figure 5.38:

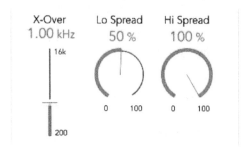

Figure 5.38: The Low Spread, Hi Spread and X-Over options in Space Designer.

- The last section, shown in Figure 5.39, is a *Dry/Wet* section, where you can set the level of the Wet (reverberated) and the Dry (unreverberated) signal. Remember, when using two sliders that move independently, it is the ratio between the two values that matters.

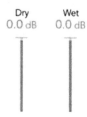

Figure 5.39: The Dry/Wet options available in Space Designer.

As an alternative to using pre-packaged impulse responses, you can instead develop your own impulse response using *SYNTHESIZED IR*.

Selecting this tab will present you with three envelopes—*Volume Env*, *Filter Env* and an additional *Density Env*, as seen in Figure 5.40:

Figure 5.40: The three envelope options available when
working with a synthesized impulse response.

- *Volume Env* works in the same way that it does on
  recorded impulse responses, except that in this situation
  you will modify noise that doesn't possess any innate
  decay information. If *Filter Env* and *Density Env* are
  switched off and a non-decaying envelope is used, the
  impulse response will therefore become a constant noise,
  as illustrated in Figure 5.41:

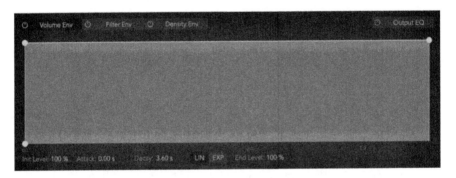

Figure 5.41: Notice the stable impulse response when no
envelopes are applied.

You can then shape this impulse response by using *Volume Env*,
as shown in Figure 5.42:

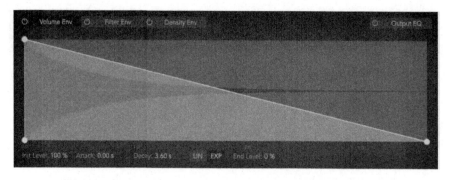

Figure 5.42: The synthesized impulse response changes in response to the envelope being applied.

- *Filter Env* shapes the frequency response over time in the same way that it does within the *SAMPLED IR* section, as shown in Figure 5.43:

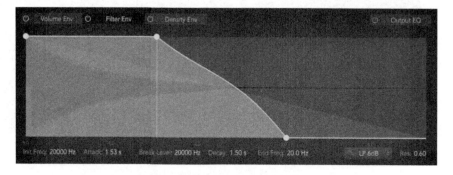

Figure 5.43: A further change occurs when a filter envelope applies to the synthesized impulse response.

Density Env, however, is a feature found in *SYNTHESIZED IR* only. This envelope has four parameters:

- *Init Density* sets the initial density. A low initial density will cause audible reflection patterns, whilst a high initial density results in a smooth initial reverb.

- *Ramp Time* sets the period between the *Initial* and *End Density* levels.

- *End Density* sets the density of the reverb tail once the ramp time has elapsed.

- The *Reflection Shape* parameter determines the gradient and intensity of early reflections. A low value will produce clustered early reflections, whilst a high value results in smooth early reflections.

The changes made in *Density Env* will be reflected in changes to the waveform. Compare for example the two impulse responses provided in Figure 5.44 and Figure 5.45 below:

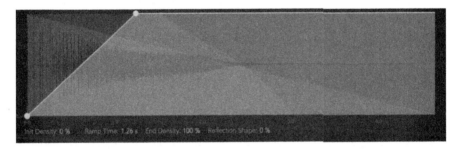

Figure 5.44: An impulse response with 0% Init Density going to 100% Init Density.

In Figure 5.44 the impulse response has been set to expand from 0% *Init Density* to 100% *End Density*. The sparse early reflections of the impulse response will probably sound grainy, and the long transition to a smooth reverb tail will sound odd, given that natural early reflections last for 50ms at most.

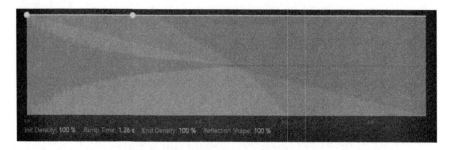

Figure 5.45: The same impulse response with 100% Init Density and 100% reflection shape.

In Figure 5.46 meanwhile, that same impulse response has been set to 100% Init Density throughout, with 100% Reflection Shape. The impulse response has no early reflections and is simply a smooth reverb tail. This will probably sound somewhat unrealistic, as our ears are used to hearing early reflections followed by late reflections.

The bottom control panel of *SYNTHESIZED IR* mode provides similar parameters to *SAMPLED IR* mode, with some key differences, as shown in Figure 5.46:

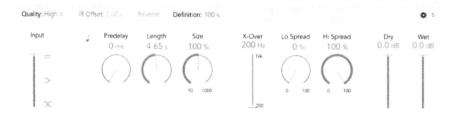

Figure 5.46: The parameters available in SYNTHESIZED IR mode.

- The *Definition* parameter allows you to select a point at which the resolution of the synthesized impulse response is reduced, saving CPU calculation resources. This means that if you set it to 50% on a 4 second impulse response,

Space Designer will use a more efficient and less complex method for calculating the last two seconds of the reverb tail than if you were to set *Definition* to 100%. This may help conserve resources if your reverb tail has already reached a near-inaudible amplitude halfway through the impulse response.

- *Lo Spread* changes the waveform of the impulse response. Unlike a sampled impulse response, a synthesized impulse response contains no natural stereo information—it must be added after the fact. *Lo Spread* achieves this by slightly delaying one channel, creating a difference between the left and right channels.

Compare the 0% *Lo Spread* impulse response in Figure 5.47 for example, with the 100% *Lo Spread* impulse response in Figure 5.48:

Figure 5.47: An impulse response with 0% Lo Spread.

Figure 5.48: An impulse response with 100% Lo Spread.

In Figure 5.48, one channel (shown in the lower half of the waveform) now starts slightly later than the other, its impulse response squeezed into a smaller amount of time than its counterpart in the upper section. This creates the artificial stereo information.

As you can see, algorithmic reverb is all about tweaking parameters to *simulate* the environment you want, whereas convolution reverb is about *using an existing environment* and tweaking it to work with your music.

The differences between algorithmic and convolution reverb are compared below, in Table 5.4.

Table 5.4: The differences between algorithmic reverb and convolution reverb.

Algorithmic reverb	Convolution reverb
Creates an artificial reverb tail using networks of delays	Creates an artificial reverb by 'convolving' a sound with a static impulse response
Can be tweaked dynamically	Must recompute when changes are made
The spaces can sound real, but physical modelling is limited to the basics	Best modelling of real spaces
More common	Less common

As reverb technology continues to advance, the lines between convolution and algorithmic reverb will blur. Ableton 11, for example, already includes a Hybrid Reverb plugin that draws upon both algorithmic and convolution techniques within a unit. It is for this reason that I have taken care to explain the ins and outs of convolution reverb; an understanding of both reverb generation techniques is helpful to get the best out of any reverb device you may encounter.

Whilst reading through this book you've been building up a large bank of theoretical knowledge and by now, you're probably eager to begin putting some of it into practice. In the next Chapter, we'll move beyond theory into some real-life experiments with reverb plugins, safe in the knowledge the contents of this Chapter can be referred to whenever the need arises.

Chapter 6: A Practical Understanding

The goal of this Chapter is to provide you with a robust understanding of reverb basics. We'll be approaching this through practical experimentation, often pushing our reverb parameters to extremes to help you gain a feel for how they can affect your sound.

To get the most out of the exercises in this Chapter, I recommend you follow along using Ableton Live's Reverb. If you don't have Ableton Live, you may wish to consider downloading a free 90-day trial version (at your own risk) from

https://www.ableton.com/en/trial/.

If you don't want to download Ableton, you will still achieve similar results from using the stock algorithmic reverb provided by the DAW of your choice.

I'll also be using a drum loop (titled Drum Loop) that you can download for free from:

https://reverb.producers.guide

Alternatively, if you prefer to work on your own material for these exercises, you can follow my written description below to create something comparable.

I also recommend using studio monitors or high-quality headphones to maximise the accuracy of your perceptions. Keeping a notebook and pen to hand will also assist you to keep track of the changes you apply to these parameters and their outcome, which can be helpful in the early stages whilst you're still getting to know your reverb plugins.

As you work through these exercises, it's a good idea to evaluate the results from the objective perspective of a someone simply listening in a room, rather than that of a music producer seeking the optimal sound. Close your eyes and picture the instruments there with you. Think about what effect the changes you make are having on the imaginary space surrounding you—does it become bigger, or smaller? Does the room sound emptier, or more filled with solid objects? Has the texture of the walls changed? Do the instruments get closer to you or further away?

6.1: Experiment One—Dry/Wet and Filtering

For this experiment, we're going to be using the sample you've downloaded, so if you would like to create this yourself, you'll need to load a non-electronic (real-sounding) drum kit into the Drum Rack instrument on Ableton (or the equivalent in your DAW) and add a conventional rock/pop drum pattern similar to the one-bar loop depicted below, in Figure 6.1. It doesn't have to be an exact copy; the important thing is that the drums sound like traditional rock/pop drums:

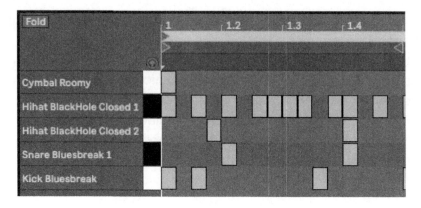

Figure 6.1: A simple drum pattern.

It's a good idea to save your work, because you'll be using this sample across several experiments within this chapter.

Now, using either your own loop or the downloaded sample, add a stock Ableton reverb as an Insert Effect on your channel, like the one shown in Figure 6.2. If you're not using Ableton, load your DAW's algorithmic reverb plugin as an Insert Effect:

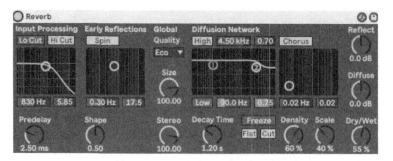

Figure 6.2: Ableton's stock reverb.

This is the default reverb configuration that loads on Ableton 10. Use Figure 6.2 to compare it with your own version just in case your default settings are any different.

Listen to your loop. Consider what information the reverb is giving you about the hypothetical environment in which the drums are being played—imagine you're listening to a real drum kit in an actual space. You might notice that it is a highly reverberant space, with reflective surfaces. There is a strange early reflection happening in the upper register and the drum kit is close by, but the walls are a medium distance away.

Now let's turn the *Dry/Wet* to 80%, as shown in Figure 6.3:

Figure 6.3: Dry/Wet set to 80%.

You'll probably notice that the drum kit seems to have moved farther away and the room sounds a little larger and more circular. This is because the closer a sound source is to us, the more of the direct sound we hear. In reducing the intensity of the direct sound by turning *Dry/Wet* to 80%, we have therefore created the impression that it is more distant.

Next, we'll bring the *Dry/Wet* right back to 15%, as shown in Figure 6.4, again listening for any changes in the perceived space:

Figure 6.4: Dry/Wet set to 15%.

At this point the drum kit is so close it sounds like you're playing it. The reflective surfaces meanwhile sound like they have moved farther away. This is because the opposite effect has now occurred and most of what you can hear is the direct sound.

Now we're going to move the *Dry/Wet* to 50% and begin experimenting with how filters can affect perception.

To start with, we'll switch off both *Lo Cut* and *Hi Cut* within the *Input Processing* section, as shown in Figure 6.5:

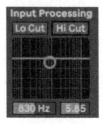

Figure 6.5: Filters switched off.

Do you notice how the surfaces of the room seem to have become more reflective? Or maybe you're perceiving that the room feels emptier, as though the soft furnishings (that absorb high frequencies) have been removed. This is because we're asking the reverb algorithm to reverberate all frequencies.

Now let's switch on *Lo Cut*, as depicted in Figure 6.6:

Figure 6.6: Lo Cut switched on, creating a high-pass filter.

If you listen carefully, you'll notice reflective material clustered towards the top half of the room. This is an interesting psychoacoustic effect driven by the preponderance of high frequencies over low frequencies.

When you turn *Hi Cut* back on, as illustrated in Figure 6.7, it sounds as though either that reflective material, or the walls of the room themselves, have been moved further away from you. This is because you are hearing a preponderance of middling frequencies now that the low and high frequencies have been removed/reduced.

Figure 6.7: Hi Cut switched on, creating a band-pass filter.

Your personal observations may have varied from those I've described so far, but I hope you've found this experiment interesting. As you've just experienced for yourself, slight changes in just one or two parameters can make a profound difference to your psychoacoustic perceptions.

6.2: Experiment Two—Size, Stereo and Reflections

For this experiment we'll be using the same drum sample as before.

We're going to begin by replacing the reverb plugin you used in Section 6.1 with a fresh one, since this is the fastest way to re-establish the default parameters that come as part of the device.

Having done this, let's change the *Quality* from *Eco* to *High*, and switch off all filtering and modulation. This will prevent modulation from interfering with the results.

The overall configuration to use is shown in Figure 6.8:

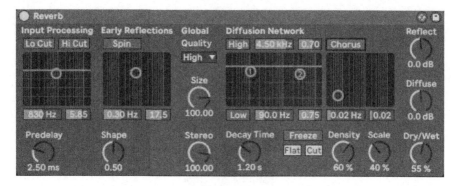

Figure 6.8: Ableton's stock reverb with High Quality and all
filtering and modulation switched off.

In this experiment we'll be experiencing the individual effects of
Size and *Stereo* and looking at how these two parameters affect
the balance between early reflections and the reverb tail itself.

With the drum track playing and the reverb active, move *Size* to its
smallest possible value (0.22), as shown in Figure 6.9, and
consider what effect it has on your perception of the space in
which the sound is being played:

Figure 6.9: Size changed to its smallest possible value.

You may feel that it's made the room sound small, like a garden
shed or a garage. This is what the algorithm is attempting to
simulate.

Now let's move *Size* to its maximum value, as shown in Figure 6.10:

Figure 6.10: Size changed to its maximum value.

You'll notice that this has made the space sound very much larger, and the reflective surfaces are now fair distance away. It's also made the reverb tail less prominent.

Next, we'll move *Size* back to its default value of 100, and change *Stereo* to 120, as shown in Figure 6.11. Can you hear how the reflective surfaces now seem farther apart, as though the size of the room has increased? You may find that this effect is similar to increasing *Dry/Wet* in the previous section.

Figure 6.11: Size at 100 and Stereo at 120.

If you turn *Stereo* to 0, as shown in Figure 6.12, you'll end up with a strange sound:

Figure 6.12: Stereo set to 0.

It's as though the entire room is composed of absorbent material, apart from a small amount of something reflective either in front of you or just behind! This is because a *Stereo* value of 0.00

removes all stereo information from the reverberation. This would be unnatural in real life since we would always hear a slightly different reverberation in each ear.

Next, we'll delve into the role played in our perceptions of reverb by both the early reflections and the reverb tail. We'll start by returning *Stereo* to its default of 100. Then we'll change *Diffuse* to its minimum of -30dB and *Reflect* to its maximum of +6dB, as shown in Figure 6.13:

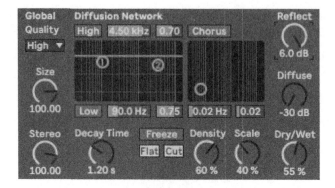

Figure 6.13: Stereo at 100, Diffuse at -30dB and Reflect at +6dB.

You are now hearing the early reflections in isolation. The result doesn't sound at all reverberated, in fact it's more like a virtual drum kit with mushy samples. This is because although early reflections form a key part of our brain's comprehension of reverberation, they must be followed by the late reflections to sound coherent to us.

Now, let's swap the two over, setting *Reflect* to -30dB and *Diffuse* to +6dB, as shown in Figure 6.14. This sounds a bit more natural, but again, it's strangely mushy, as though the angles of the room don't quite make sense.

Figure 6.14: Reflect at -30dB and Diffuse at +6dB.

Finally, we'll change *Reflect* to +6dB to match *Diffuse*, like in Figure 6.15. Do you notice how the room suddenly makes audial sense again?

Figure 6.15: Both Reflect and Diffuse at +6dB.

The purpose of this experiment has been to show the importance of the conjunction between early reflections and the reverb tail. Together they form an integral feature of our psychoacoustic perception of reverberation; if one of these two components is missing, the resulting sound will be unnatural, poorly defined, and unrealistic.

Now let's move on to our next experiment: modulation.

6.3: Experiment Three—Modulation

In this experiment, we'll look at how modulation affects both the early reflections and the reverb tail.

Maintaining our settings from Experiment Two, we'll bring *Diffuse* down to 0dB, but keep *Reflect* at +6dB. The overall configuration to use is as shown in Figure 6.16:

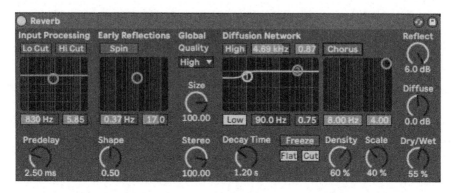

Figure 6.16: The starting configuration for Experiment Three.

Listen carefully to the result. You'll notice that the reflections seem to move faster. This is because our perception merges the early reflections with the late reflections. By combining the two, the cascade in intensity across the reverb tail seems to occur more rapidly.

Now turn on *Spin* and place the *Early Reflections* XY controller into the top-right of the XY control, as shown in Figure 6.17. This will create the fastest, most prominent early reflection modulation possible:

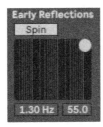

Figure 6.17: Maximisation of the speed and prominence of early reflections.

This modulation produces variations in the early reflections that seem to transform the room, from one with a simple shape to something much more architecturally complicated.

Next, we'll turn our attention to the late reflections. Under *Chorus* we'll set the maximum amounts possible for both modulation and frequency.

Change *Reflect* to 0dB and *Diffuse* to +6dB, as shown in Figure 6.18:

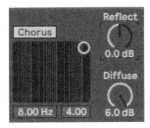

Figure 6.18: Reflect set to 0dB and Diffuse set to +6dB.

Can you hear the increased complexity of the perceived space? If you listen closely, you may even detect patterns in the modulation's shifting, giving it an unnatural feel. This is because of its intensity. If you want to create a complex picture for your listener therefore, the correct balance to aim for will be one with sufficient modulation to allow the elements of randomness to be present, but not to the extent that the process of modulation itself becomes noticeable.

6.4: Experiment Four—Reverb Tail Filtering

For the fourth experiment, we're going to look at how a reverb tail filter affects our perception of the surrounding space.

We'll start by setting the reverb configuration to those shown in Figure 6.19. You won't need to reload the plugin to do this:

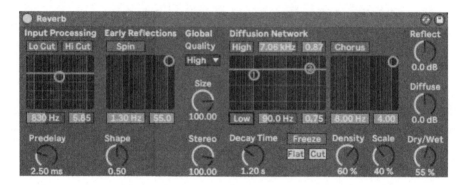

Figure 6.19: The starting Reverb configuration for Experiment Four.

To establish a baseline, first play the loop through the reverb unit set to this configuration (Figure 6.19). Now switch on *High* within the diffusion network, setting the frequency to roughly 1.5kHz and the level to 1.00, as shown in Figure 6.20:

Figure 6.20: The Diffusion Network, with High switched on and set to a frequency of 1.5kHz.

Whilst monitoring the sound, move the level of this filter downwards, as shown in Figure 6.21, from 1.00 to 0.20:

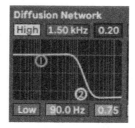

Figure 6.21: High switched on, with the level reduced to 0.20.

As you bring it downwards, you'll probably hear the sparkle of the reverb dimming, and the perceived size and reflectivity of the room will reduce.

Leaving *High* switched on, now switch on *Low*, as shown in Figure 6.22, setting the frequency to 200Hz:

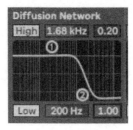

Figure 6.22: The High and Low switched on, with the frequency at 200Hz.

With your loop still playing through the reverb, slowly reduce the volume of *Low*. You will notice the environment becoming even smaller, until it sounds like a single reflective plate in front of you, placed within a non-reflective room.

For the next stage of our experiment, switch off *High* altogether, as shown in Figure 6.23, so that your reverb tail excludes the lower frequencies:

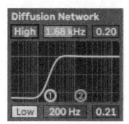

Figure 6.23: High switched off.

You might now hear the higher frequencies fizzing around the space. This produces a bright, present sound, but one that is unnatural, because high frequencies rarely reverberate in isolation in real life.

6.5: Experiment Five—Decay Time

For the fifth and final experiment, we're going to see what happens when we tweak the decay time. You won't need to reload the plugin for this. We'll begin by turning off all filters and modulation, whilst keeping all other parameters at their default settings, using the configuration shown below in Figure 6.24:

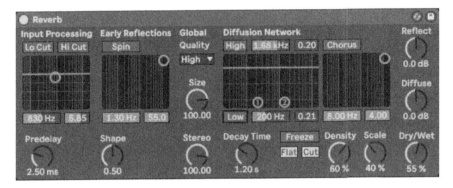

Figure 6.24: The configuration used for Experiment Five.

First put the *Decay Time* at its lowest setting, of 200ms.

Now gradually turn *Decay Time* upwards to 60s and note the changes along the way.

Here are some of my own observations:

- 200ms: There's very little discernible reverberation present.

- 300ms: Some slight reflectivity, as though the drums are being played in a well-treated studio.

- 400ms: Higher reflectivity, with audible reflections of the snare becoming apparent.

- 500ms: The snare's reflection has become more prominent.

- 600ms: Clearer reverberation is present, with the kickdrum becoming prominent.

- 700ms: The room sounds small, but highly reflective.

- 1s: The room sounds large and the room's material is becoming more reflective.

- 1.4s: Individual drum hits are less discernible within the reflections.

- 1.6s: Too much reflectivity, everything is sounding smeared.

- 2s: The reflections are noisy and over-energetic.

- 2.5s: The reverb is now completely lacking in definition.

- 3s: The reverb sounds confusing and disordered.

- 4s: The reverb is messy and unpleasant to listen to.

- 5s: There's very little rhythm left in the reverb tail.

- 7.5s: The reverb has become a noisy, disorganised shambles.

Chapter 7: Reverb in Action

Having experienced for yourself the impact that reverb devices can have on a sound, it's now time to examine their application within the specific context of music production.

Because reverb is such a universal psychoacoustic phenomenon, a very broad range of approaches can be employed for its use. How prescriptive you want to be therefore will depend on your goals. You could aim to give your track more space. You might want your music to emulate the standards of tracks that you admire. You may even wish to create a unique signature sound, or explore the outer limits of what's possible with reverb.

Your skill using reverb as a producer will come from combining your understanding of the underlying theory—as outlined in this book—with the practical experience gained from applying reverb across a variety of situations.

As a starting point for the practice element, let's look at some helpful guiding principles that can have an immediate, positive impact on your music production.

7.1.1: Auxiliary tracks

Auxiliary, or aux tracks (as described in Chapter 1 of this book) are a great way to work with reverb.

Whilst you can reverberate tracks by using Insert Effects, or even use reverb as a Master Effect, many producers choose to reverberate using aux tracks. The primary advantages of doing so are listed below:

- Sending instruments to a reverb unit with a single set of parameters places them within the same sonic 'space', creating a sense of psychoacoustic realism.

- Using aux tracks saves time, since you can hear the results of any reverb that you add without having to configure each individual track's reverb.

- An aux track enables you change the volume of all the reverberation sent through it in one action.

- You can add effects (such as distortion or compression etc.) to the sound of your reverb.

- Aux tracks save CPU, which is a great help if your computer has processing constraints.

Because aux tracks are routed to the main output, reverbs on aux tracks should always be set to 100% Wet, otherwise the dry signal on the auxiliary track will duplicate the tracks that you send there, making the levels difficult to control.

Ableton Live 10 provides an aux track that is already set up for reverb by default, although you will naturally want to adapt the parameters of this reverb when you use it. In Ableton, an aux track is called a *Return Track*. Figure 7.1 shows three Ableton tracks being 'sent' to aux channel A:

Figure 7.1: Auxiliary tracks in Ableton.

You don't need to restrict yourself to a single aux track, but it's worth using the same aux track for layers that you'd expect to share a single sonic space, for example:

- An aux track for fast-attacking layers, like snares, hi-hats, keyboards, or vocal verses.

- An aux track for slower layers, such as strings or pads.

To set up a new aux track in Ableton, right-click in *Arrange View* and select *Insert Return Track*, as shown in Figure 7.2:

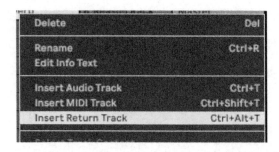

Figure 7.2: How to insert a Return Track in Ableton.

Since Ableton reserves numbers for Audio and MIDI tracks, your new *Return track* will be allocated an alphabetical track designation. You can then 'send' audio to the *Return track* using the corresponding *Send* pots. For example, the track depicted in Figure 7.3 is 'sending' the maximum amount of audio to *Return track A*, and roughly half that amount to *Return track B*:

Figure 7.3: Two Sends in Ableton Live.

When using Logic to set up an aux track, the terminology you'll use is *Bus track*. You may remember from Chapter 1 that an *Aux track* is a type of *Bus track*, and that what differentiates the two is that an Aux track can send a variable amount of signal to an effects device.

To set up an auxiliary track in Logic, you will need to follow these steps:

1. Under *'Audio FX'* on your track, click on the *Send* button, as shown at the bottom of Figure 7.4:

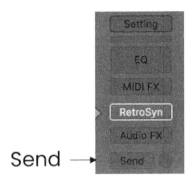

Send →

Figure 7.4: The Send button in Logic Pro X is at the bottom of this picture.

2. Select an available *Bus* from the drop-down menu (Bus 1, for example) as shown in Figure 7.5:

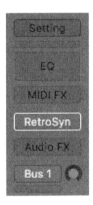

Figure 7.5: A Bus track selected.

3. You'll see that a new track has automatically been created to the right, as shown in Figure 7.6. This is a *Bus track*.

Figure 7.6: A Bus track.

4. You can then add your reverb to the effects rack for this new *bus track*, as shown in Figure 7.7:

Figure 7.7: A Bus track with ChromaVerb added.

Remember to set your reverb to 100% *Wet* and 0% *Dry*, so that you don't accidentally duplicate your dry signal by sending it to the *Bus*.

5. If you want to add this *Bus track* to your main window, Ctrl-click on it and select *Create Track*, as shown in Figure 7.8:

Figure 7.8: Adding a Bus track to the main window on Logic Pro X.

Now that you've set up your aux track and routed to it the tracks you want reverberated, it's time to consider the next step in the workflow: achieving the right reverb settings.

7.1.2: The lower end

Whilst experimenting with reverb devices, you may have noticed that low frequency instruments can sound muddy, particularly when playing frequencies below 250Hz. It is for this reason that producers often utilise bass instruments without applying reverb to them at all. That's not to say that you shouldn't use reverb on bass instruments, but to get the best results you will need to be selective as to which frequencies you target, aiming for the higher harmonics. Adding reverb to the upper harmonics of an instrument such as a kickdrum, bass guitar or Roland 303 for example, can provide it with greater presence in the mix.

The best way to go about this is to add a high-pass filter before your reverb on your aux channel, to attenuate the lowest frequencies. Look at the EQ display in Figure 7.9 below, where the lowest two harmonics of this bass instrument have been filtered— seen here as distinct peaks within the frequency analyser:

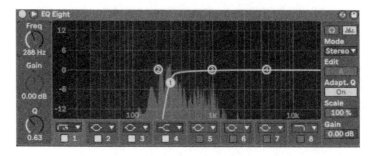

Figure 7.9: The lowest two harmonics removed from a bass instrument, preventing its lowest frequencies from being reverberated.

If, despite the risks, you choose to reverberate the lower end, make the reverb's input mono (that is, zero stereo) using a *Utility* device and set your reverb to zero *Width*, as shown in Figure 7.10:

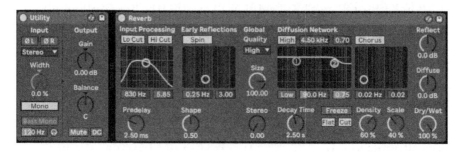

Figure 7.10: A reverb's source material made mono using Utility. Note the Mono button activated, followed by the reverb itself made Mono by setting Stereo to zero.

The reason for this is that the lower end of your mix often needs clarity, and too much stereo information can make it sound murky. If you're pressing your music to vinyl, too much low-end stereo information can cause the needle to skip on the vinyl record, so your mastering engineer will probably remove that stereo information to prevent mix issues, thereby negating your work.

7.1.3: Room treatment

Not all of us have the benefit of access to a music studio with well thought-out acoustic treatment and high-quality studio monitors.

If you're not working in a professional studio or a treated room (meaning one that has been set up acoustically for optimal sound reproduction) it's wise to alternate between using headphones and studio monitors to assess your reverb. This is because an untreated room will reverberate the output of your monitors off the walls and ceiling. These natural room reverberations will coalesce with the artificial reverberations in your mix, making it harder to set your parameters. Headphones, meanwhile, will not give you an accurate stereo image, because there's no interaction between the sound coming from the left and right speakers in your headphones and the air. You will therefore receive an extreme sense of directionality.

The best compromise in the absence of a professionally treated studio is to use headphones for decay and texture and to use monitors for stereo image and frequency choice. Once you've done that, make your last checks using both headphones and monitors.

Of course, if you're working in a high-quality music studio, monitors alone will suffice.

7.1.4: Space

When setting up your reverb, it's important to apply an overarching logic to the psychoacoustic 'spaces' you create. Whilst you don't need to restrict yourself to a single space in a track, too many reverb units with too many sonic environments will create a confusing mix, as the listener's ear will perceive many contradictory environments. If you are creating smaller, more intimate acoustic environments where you will often use shorter decay times, some of the confusion resulting from overlapping sonic environments can be mitigated by reducing the amount of high frequency content present, because high frequency overlaps are the element that will be most prominent to your listener.

Instruments of a similar category should occupy similar spaces. A good way to go about this is to send instruments of comparable sonic character to a single aux channel with a short reverb. In Figure 7.11 for example, several drum layers have been sent to an aux reverb channel (channel A to the right of the image). This channel is so quiet that it cannot be heard as part of the mix; in fact, the only way it can be perceived is that something sounds as though it's missing when it's muted. Despite being barely audible, this auxiliary reverb will give the mix an essential cohesiveness:

Figure 7.11: A quiet auxiliary reverb, creating cohesiveness within the mix.

Remember to apply the concept of space to samples, too. Pre-packaged samples and loops are intentionally provided 'dry', with no effects added, whereas sounds are rarely 'dry' in real life. A small amount of reverb is essential to bring these samples to life.

If your aim is realism, think carefully about the environmental context in which your recorded instruments would be most likely to be played. It's probable that an orchestra would be heard in an orchestral chamber for example, so a chamber reverb would be appropriate for such tracks. A punk band might typically be heard in a smaller venue, so a basic room reverb might provide the most authentic feel.

Another vital element to consider when creating your psychoacoustic space is your placement of the various sound sources within it. In music production, this is achieved through panning, whereby sounds are moved to the left or right of the stereo field. When used with panning, reverb can work well to create the feeling of a three-dimensional space, and it's therefore important to regard reverb and panning as counterparts to one another when placing your instruments. Lesser amounts of reverb will keep instruments to the front of the area and closer to the listener, whilst greater amounts of reverb will move instruments farther from the listener, more toward the back of the room.

This kind of space is illustrated in Figure 7.12:

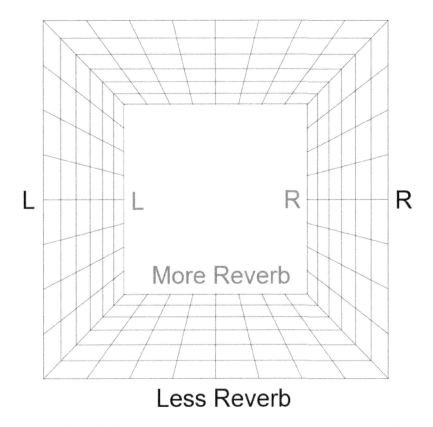

L   L   R   R

More Reverb

Less Reverb

Figure 7.12: A three-dimensional space created by panning and reverberation extent.

The placement of your instruments is of particular importance when realism is your goal. If you're mixing a band for example, think about where the musicians would be physically standing on that stage, and don't accidentally put your back-up singers in front of your main vocalist, or your lead guitar behind your drums!

If you're mixing a drum track, examine the positions of the snare, the kick, the hi-hat, and the auxiliary percussion such as shakers and tambourines. In doing so, you'll achieve more clarity because each instrument will occupy its own discrete spot in the stereo field.

7.1.5: Suitability

Whether your aim is to create realistic spaces or artificial ones, the suitability of the reverb within the broader context of the overall mix should always be of primary consideration. Remember that more aggressive instruments—such as drums or piano—will become washed out by longer decay times and therefore need shorter decay. Less aggressive instruments such as pads will need a longer decay to allow the individual notes to merge in a way that is fluent and pleasing.

Always double check to ensure your panning is coherent; an instrument and its reverberation should be panned in a similar way to one another. Echoes from an instrument placed to the left of a room for example, will be heard predominantly from the left side of that room. On many stereo reverbs, this will happen by default, but it is worth making sure that you haven't accidentally panned your auxiliary channel to the opposite side from your instrument.

7.1.6: Summary

Below, is a summary of the five tips outlined in this chapter:

1. Use auxiliary tracks. They speed up your workflow, increase realism and save CPU.

2. Do not reverberate lower frequencies (particularly below 250Hz). They create a muddy sound. Reverberate their upper harmonics instead.

3. In the absence of a professionally treated studio, use headphones and studio monitors to assess your reverb. Use headphones for decay and texture and monitors for stereo image and frequency choice.

4. Instruments of a similar character should occupy a similar reverberant 'space'.

5. Consider the realism and suitability of the 'space' that you create in terms of decay times and panning.

With these grounding principles in mind, we can move to the next section, where we will break down the application of reverb into systematic steps, allowing you to achieve significant results whilst further building your knowledge.

7.2: An All-Purpose Workflow

The sheer number of parameters available across reverb units can be daunting. If your reverb unit has 24 different parameters for example, and you can only change one at a time, you could approach your reverb unit in over 500 different ways. To simplify things, I've therefore devised a systematic workflow that is applicable to any reverb unit. Consistent and repeated use of this workflow will enable you to gain a deeper understanding of the art of applying reverb, thereby improving your experience, and speeding up your decision-making processes.

Before implementing this workflow, it's a good idea to double check that the auxiliary track to which you've added your reverb is turned to 100% Wet, since failure to do so can produce less than optimal results!

There are three stages to this workflow: Time, Texture and Finishing Touches.

Let's begin with Time:

1. Set the *quality* to as high as possible.

2. Set the *decay time*. Turn it higher until your reverb sounds washed out, then bring the values back down to the point where it creates a pleasant sonic space. Listen carefully to your *decay time* and try to adjust it to match the rhythm and tempo of the track.

3. Set the *size*. Again, start higher and work downwards. Think about what kind of space you want your sound to occupy. Start by setting the *size* of the main reverb tail, and then—if you have the option—tailor the *size* of the *early reflections* to fit with this tail.

4. Set the *predelay*. It's a good idea to be conservative with this (5-50ms) unless you're aiming for a specific effect.

5. Revisit the *decay time*. Make smaller tweaks to find the sweet spot. Move back to *size* if necessary.

Now you can move on to Texture:

6. Tweak the *diffusion* and/or *density* to create the right texture. Think about whether you want it bright or dark, dense or diffuse.

7. Set the *modulation* on both early reflections and the reverb tail. More *modulation* means more colour, and increased colour draws attention to the reverb tail itself. Do you want your reverb tail to capture your listeners' attention, or just provide background atmosphere?

8. Set the balance between early reflections and reverb tail (unless you're already happy with it).

9. Set the *input and output filters,* reviewing how this changes the character of the reverb tail. If you have soloed the auxiliary track at some point, make sure you also review it within the overall context of your mix.

10. Change the amount of *stereo* to create the stereo image you want. I recommend employing a wider stereo image when you're using multiple instruments, and on all naturally wide instruments, such as pads. Conversely, single instruments—such as one guitar for example—will usually sound better with a narrower stereo image.

Finally, you can apply the Finishing Touches:

11. Tweak the amount of each layer that you're sending to the reverb auxiliary channel.

12. Experiment with external effects on your aux track, such as distortion or compression.

Time and Texture, the two parts of the workflow that occur within your reverb plugin, are process illustrated on Ableton's Reverb in Figure 7.13:

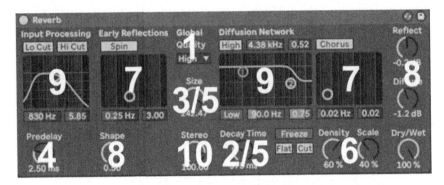

Figure 7.13: The all-purpose reverb workflow illustrated on Ableton's Reverb.

It may be the case that your reverb plugin doesn't contain all the above parameters, but that doesn't mean you can't follow this workflow—just make sure you *tweak time before texture*. Depending on the algorithm or impulse responses in use, the nonlinearities within reverb tails mean that time can change the character of your reverb tail, which will force you to start again if your changes to time result in the wrong texture.

The next section contains slight variations on the above workflow, tweaked for application to specific instruments.

7.3 Specific Instruments

In this section we'll be looking at some prescriptive methods that work well with particular instruments. These are tried-and-tested techniques that will quickly improve your use of reverb and can provide a good starting point for more creative approaches.

Reverb works well on instruments of a similar duration and texture, so it's worth considering other instruments that a particular technique might also be suitable for. One that works well on drums may also work well on a fast-moving synth with lots of treble, for example. It will not work so well on a slow pad, however.

7.3.1: Drums

Comprising a variety of sounds, each with their own unique qualities, the objectives when reverberating drums differ from those for other instruments. Ideally you should aim to apply reverb in such a way as to create ambience, whilst still preserving the percussive character of the individual sounds.

When reverberating drums, you can use the same three-stage approach previously outlined, with the proviso that you make allowances for the type of sound that you will reverberate:

1. Set the reverb to 100% *Wet* (or turn the *Dry* signal off).

2. Set the *quality* as high as possible.

3. Don't use reverb on the kickdrum. If you've got multiple tracks for your drum layers, minimise the amount of reverb sent from the kick to the reverb. If all your drums are on a single track, EQ the reverb input to remove lower frequencies.

You can now start considering Time:

4. Set an initial *decay time* at 1/4 of a bar. To calculate this, divide your BPM by 60, then divide 1000 by that number. For example, if your track is 160BPM track, divide it by 60, which gives you 2.66. 1000 divided by 2.66 is 375, so you would use 375ms as your initial *decay time*. This will provide your reverb with rhythmic interest. If this decay time is too long, try halving that number again. In this instance, that would mean reducing it to 187.5ms (because $375 \div 2 = 187.5$).

5. Set the size. Again, start higher and work downwards. Think about the space you want to portray.

6. Set the *predelay*. It's a good idea to be conservative here and choose something in the 2.5-25ms range.

Now turn your attention to Texture:

7. Tweak the *diffusion* and/or *density* to create the most suitable texture for your sound.

8. Set the *modulation* on both early reflections and the reverb tail. For a more natural sound, you may wish to dial the *modulation* down on drum reverb tails.

9. Set the balance between the early reflections and the reverb tail. A large degree of early reflections will give your drums a direct sound at the expense of clarity, whereas a lower degree of early reflections may sound unnatural and detract from the rhythm, so you will be aiming for a sweet spot between those two extremes.

10. Change the amount of *stereo* to create the stereo image you want. With percussion, I'd recommend a narrow stereo image, to contrast with other layers in the track that possess a wider reverb stereo image, such as vocals.

11. Add a low-pass filter of between 4kHz and 10kHz to the reverb tail. This is to prevent too much unnatural 'fizz' being added to your hi-hats, since these high frequencies are absorbed more quickly in the air.

Now for the Finishing Touches:

12. Set the amount of each layer that you're sending to the reverb.

13. Experiment with external effects on your aux track, such as distortion or compression.

An example drum reverb configuration based on the above workflow is shown in Figure 7.14 (the track is at 124BPM):

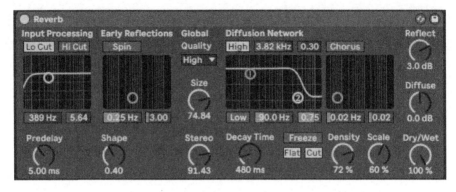

Figure 7.14: An example drum reverb configuration.

Besides the reverb you've just set, there is a secret weapon that you can deploy! This involves adding an extra auxiliary channel with a very quiet background reverb set to a long decay time. Keep the levels of this reverb very low. It should be so subdued that the reverb tails can't be heard in the mix and the only way to tell they're there at all is to hear a slight loss of presence when the auxiliary track is muted. An example settings suitable for such an aux track is shown in Figure 7.15:

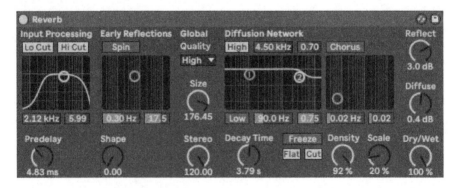

Figure 7.15: An example configuration of an additional, quiet, auxiliary reverb.

Whilst your drums will gain most of their presence through use of the shorter reverb, this almost undetectable longer reverb can sometimes add a certain ambience, enabling them to stand out in the mix that bit more.

Next, we'll look at a specific workflow for your melody and harmony instruments, such as a piano, guitar, or synthesizer.

7.3.2: Melodic Instruments

The principle of creating two sonic spaces for your instruments to occupy can work just as well for melodic instruments as it does for drums, but this time you will be inverting the process: most of the presence will come from the longer reverb, which is then enhanced by a small, almost sub-audible amount of additional rhythmic reverb. Items 1. and 2. below describe this process in greater detail.

1. Begin by adding a very light reverb to an aux track and send a low amount of all your instruments to this channel, so that the reverb can barely be heard within the wider context of your mix. This will be the almost sub-audible reverb mentioned above, and its purpose is purely to add ambience. Aim for a fairly quiet Aux channel with a 100% wet reverb, set to a short *predelay*, a short *decay* of between 300 and 600ms, and a small room *size*. Your settings should look fairly like the configuration shown in Figure 7.16:

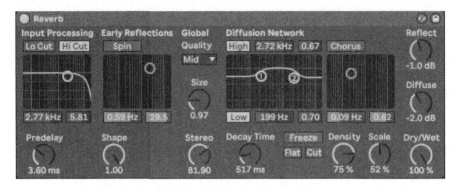

Figure 7.16: A light, slight reverb configuration.

Please be aware that this reverb adds subtle atmospheric elements, so if your instruments were originally recorded in a reverberant environment this effect will already be in place. Sending them to this aux channel would therefore be unnecessary and could cause your listener some psychoacoustic confusion.

2. Pair this initial reverb with a longer instrument reverb, by creating a new auxiliary track, adding a reverb plugin and sending a substantial degree of your instruments to it. Use the All-Purpose Workflow in section 7.2 to craft the character of the virtual space you wish to create.

3. Now add EQ to the auxiliary channel of this secondary reverb, so that the output of this reverb is EQ'd. You might like to try using the Abbey Road EQ trick for this, a reverb EQ that has been employed to great success since the 1960s. For this technique, set a high-pass filter to cut everything under 600Hz with a 12dB or 18dB/octave slope, and then set a low-pass filter to cut everything above 10kHz. An example of this is shown in Figure 7.17:

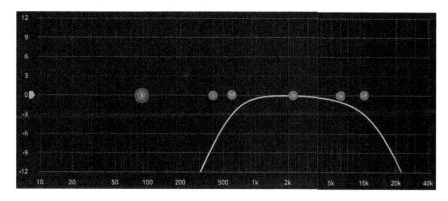

Figure 7.17: The Abbey Road EQ.

The Abbey Road trick will clean up your reverb considerably, giving you space to add more ambience without washing out your mix.

4. If at this point you wish to draw attention to your reverb or add some harmonic grit, then you might find it helpful to add Saturation or Distortion to your aux track (after your EQ) such as the saturation shown in Figure 7.18:

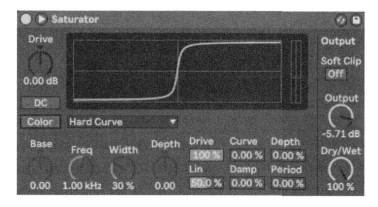

Figure 7.18: An example of a Saturation configuration that could be added to your reverb.

If you don't want to draw attention to your reverb, try tightening the frequency range of the Abbey Road EQ you used in Step 3.

Next, we'll look at an approach for reverberating vocals within the context of a mix.

7.3.3: Vocals

As with the previous workflows, I recommend using an auxiliary track for your reverb.

It is important to be judicious when reverberating vocals since they tend to work best when placed front and centre. As you will recall from our experiments in Chapter 6, this positioning means that less reverb will be required.

It can be helpful to use a warm, characterful reverb to highlight the vocals. I'd recommend either:

- A plate reverb simulation, or a plate reverb using convolution.

- A warm setting using a top-class algorithmic reverb such as ValhallaRoom.

Alternatively, if you don't have access to either of these, you can use your DAW's stock reverb.

1. Just like the other workflows, set the reverb to 100% *Wet* (or turn the *Dry* signal off).

---

2. Set the *quality* as high as possible if your plugin has that function.

3. Consider using a shorter *decay time* that keeps the vocalist's articulation of the lyrics intact, such as one between 0.5 and 1.5 seconds.

4. Start at a high *Size* and work downwards until the reverb has the level of intimacy that you wish.

5. Lengthen the *predelay time* until the reverb sits slightly distinct from the vocal. This will normally be around 25-100ms.

6. Carefully balance the early reflections with the reverb tail level. More early reflections create intimacy, but this will be at the expense of lushness. Conversely, more reverb tail will create lushness, but at the expense of intimacy.

7. Tweak the *diffusion* and/or *density* to create the desired texture.

8. Add some modulation if required but go easy on it if you're looking for realism.

9. Change the *stereo* to the stereo image you want. On lead vocals, you can generally use a high *stereo* parameter to create a strong stereo image.

10. To preserve the clarity of the lyrics, it's important to separate your vocals from their reverb tail. The first step is to use an Abbey Road EQ on the reverb, following the same technique outlined for a melodic instrument (a high-pass above 600Hz and a low-pass below 10kHz).

11. Now add a second EQ and locate the lowest two peaks on the frequency analyser. These will generally be the fundamental and first harmonics. Since these define the vocal, you'll want them to receive less reverberation than the higher harmonics. To achieve

this, you can reduce their intensity using EQ. Then try decreasing the intensity of some of the top end, so that the air and sibilance of the vocals don't take too much of the listener's focus. The result is shown in Figure 7.19:

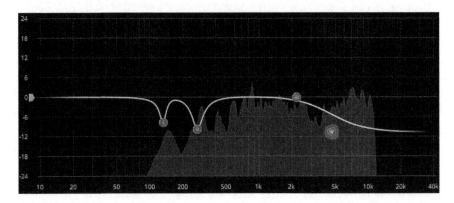

Figure 7.19: A vocal with the first two harmonics and the top end EQ'd out.

12. If you want your vocal to occupy the centre of the stereo space, you may find it helpful to push the reverberation out to the sides of the stereo field. To accomplish this, you will need to isolate the stereo information using mid-side processing. You can achieve this in Ableton by adding a Utility to your reverb aux channel. Right-click on *Width* and click on *Mid/Side Mode*, as depicted in Figure 7.20:

the examples illustrated below I've used a drum clip to demonstrate the process.

To create a reversed reverb tail in Ableton, follow these steps (which will be broadly similar across other DAWs):

1. Make sure you have *Loop* turned off on the clip to which you want to apply reverse reverberation. You may find it helpful to use your clip as a distinct audio sample that can be triggered. Alternatively, you could record a MIDI clip with the sample already triggered.

2. In *Arrange* view, create a new Audio track. Send the output of the track with the sample to the input of this new Audio track. Set the Audio track's *Monitor* to *In*, as seen in Figure 8.1:

Figure 8.1: The Audio track on the right has its Monitor set to In.

3. Add a reverb as an insert effect to the track you intend to reverberate, and then configure the reverb unit to your preference. Think about texture, stereo information and decay time, remembering that you're looking for a decay time that will slot well into your track. Consider making the reverb 100% *Wet* or close to it, like the reverb in Figure 8.2:

Figure 8.2: A reverb with high Wet.

4. *Record-enable* the track on which you intend to record the reverberated sample, as shown in Figure 8.3:

Figure 8.3: A record-enabled audio track.

5. Set your *Quantization* to at least 1 Bar. This is to ensure that you record the sample accurately and avoid having to edit it later. You can see this shown to the right, on Figure 8.4:

Figure 8.4: The quantisation set to 1 Bar.

6. With all *Clips* disabled, press *Play* on the main *Arrange View* playhead. To ensure that your Audio track records while your sample plays, trigger the *Record* button on your Audio track and then trigger your sample within the same quantization period. My drum sample and the recording channel are shown together in Figure 8.5:

Figure 8.5: Clips to trigger. Try to ensure that your audio track records at the same time as the sample plays.

7. Wait until the reverb tail has completely ceased. You'll be able to tell this from the levels on the Audio track's meter.

8. Set the Audio track's *Audio From* to *No Input* and the *Monitor* to *Auto*, as shown in Figure 8.6. You should also change the *Audio To* of your sample to *Master*, unless you want to record more reverb tails:

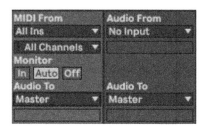

Figure 8.6: The Monitor set to Auto.

9. Double-click on the reverberated sample you just created. Click on *Rev* to reverse it. You can also increase the clip volume should you wish, as shown in Figure 8.7:

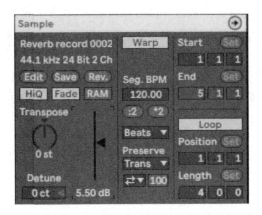

Figure 8.7: Sample settings. Click on Rev. to reverse the reverb.

And that's it! You can drop this reversed reverb sample anywhere in your track and save it for future use.

To create a reversed reverb in Logic, you can use Logic Pro X's Space Designer's convolution reverb to create a reverse impulse response. This is done by loading a reverb template and clicking on the *Reverse* button. If you find have empty air at the start of the impulse response, you can use the *Envelope* to cut it, as shown in Figure 8.8:

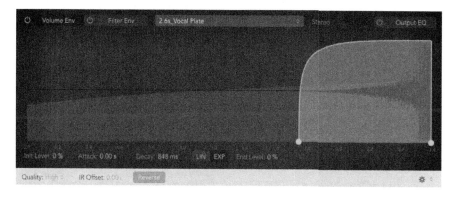

Figure 8.8: A reversed impulse response in Space Designer, using the envelope to cut the empty air at the start of the IR.

Instead, however, I recommend using the same method described for Ableton: creating a copy of your reverberated sound and reversing that, because it will give you more control over the outcome. You can do this using Logic's ChromaVerb by following these steps:

1. Create a MIDI clip with the sound you want to reverberate and reverse, such as an Ultrabeat drum hit, as depicted in Figure 8.9:

Figure 8.9: A MIDI clip triggering the sound we want to reverse.

2. Add your reverb as an Insert Effect. Remember to make it bright and wet, with a long reverb tail, as shown in ChromaVerb, Figure 8.10:

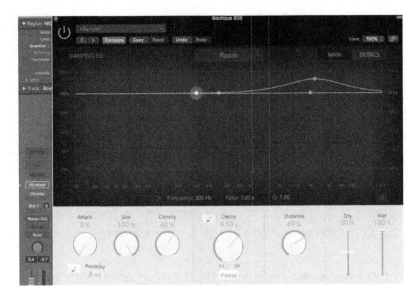

Figure 8.10: ChromaVerb configured to create a bright, long reverb tail.

3. Play your reverberated drum hit. The reverb tail should finish before the end of the clip.

4. Right-click on the MIDI clip and click on *Bounce In Place*, as depicted in Figure 8.11:

Figure 8.11: The Bounce in Place function in Logic Pro X.

5. Select *Leave* under the source menu unless you're certain
    that you'll get it perfect on your first try. The other settings
    to use are shown in Figure 8.12:

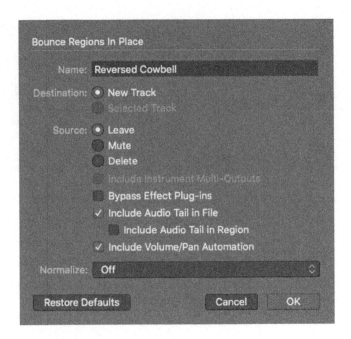

Figure 8.12: The settings to consider using when using Bounce in Place.

6. Click on your newly recorded clip, then click on File, then go to *Functions -> Reverse*, as shown in Figure 8.13:

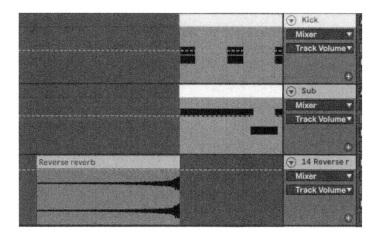

Figure 8.13: How to reverse an audio clip in Logic.

7. Solo your reversed reverb and audition it. If you find that it needs to be adjusted, you can tweak the initial track (that you left in place) and then bounce it in place again.

The technical aspect of creating a reverse reverb is easy once you've practised it a few times and provides the advantage of offering many interesting possibilities. You could, for example:

- Use a long Decay Time with high *Stereo* on a crash cymbal or vocal, creating a big, dramatic riser.

- Use a short decay time on a snare drum or hi-hat, adding this to your drum kit.

- Create a warped reversed reverb, adding distortion or bitcrushing to your reversed reverb sample.

- Timestretch your reversed reverb.

- Add multiple layers to the input of the Audio track you plan to reverse.

- Reverberate a sound or texture already used in your track, making it sound like part of a layer.

- Automate the envelope of the reversed reverb to create a more dramatic riser.

- Reverberate your reversed reverb, for added drama.

In the example shown in Figure 8.14 below, I've used a reversed reverb as a transitional tool. Notice how the reverse reverb peaks just as the kick and sub-bass come in:

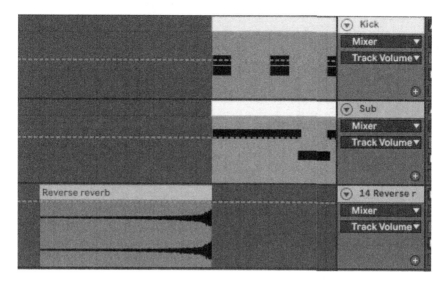

Figure 8.14: The use of reverse reverb to create a transition. The reverse reverb is at the bottom of the three tracks.

Reverse reverb is an extremely powerful effect. Used sparingly, it can create highly distinctive effects that add drama and intrigue to your work.

Next, we'll look at a powerful technique that has been in use since the 1980s: gated reverb.

8.2: Gated Reverb

Reverb tails naturally decay. An example is shown in Figure 8.15:

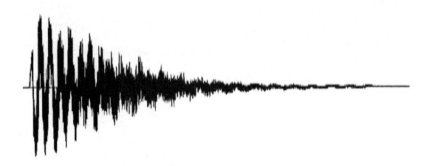

Figure 8.15: The natural decay of a reverb tail.

Let's imagine that you wanted to capture the intensity of a long reverb tail, but only have it last a short time, such as the length of a single beat. Ordinarily, it wouldn't be possible to shorten a reverb tail without drastically curtailing its decay time, which would also remove its intensity. The way to overcome this dilemma is through using a Gate.

A Gate is a device that only allows sounds through if they reach a certain loudness threshold. It significantly attenuates all signals below that threshold. Imagine a threshold applied to a passage of music, like the one shown in Figure 8.16 for example:

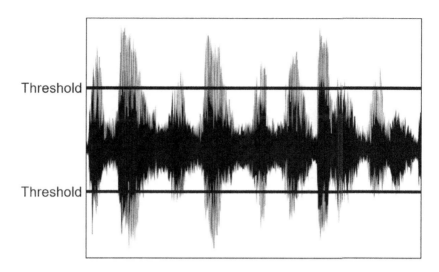

Figure 8.16: A hypothetical threshold applied to a passage of music.

Since a Gate would essentially refuse to let through any audio that didn't meet the threshold, the resulting audio wave would look stuttered, like the one in Figure 8.17. These abrupt ends would mean the sound of the reverb would be cut off:

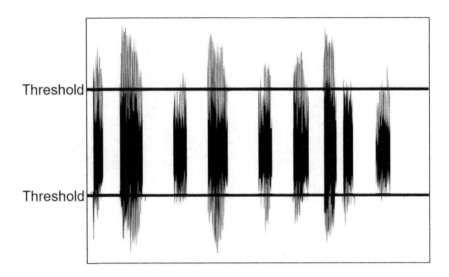

Figure 8.17: How the same passage of music would look with a Gate applied.

This gating technique can create some fascinating reverb effects. Imagine these same thresholds applied to a reverb tail, as shown in Figure 8.18:

Figure 8.18: Gate thresholds applied to a reverb tail.

With the Gate in place, the reverb tail would now look like the one shown in Figure 8.19—short, sharp, and intense, with a reverb tail that ends artificially early:

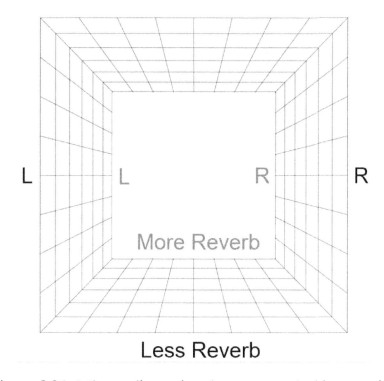

L   L   R   R

More Reverb

Less Reverb

Figure 8.34: A three-dimensional space created by panning and reverberation extent.

By altering the prominence of musical elements within a track whilst it plays, you can affect the listener's perceptions of how close or distant those elements are, creating a sense of progression and change. The uppermost synth line shown below in Figure 8.35 for example, first moves away from the listener and then back toward them. This was achieved by automating the amount of reverb sent to the auxiliary channel:

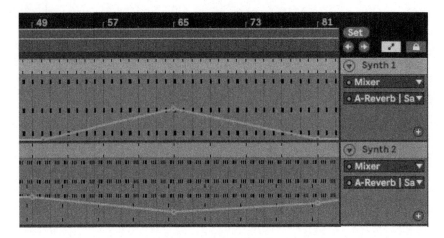

Figure 8.35: Two synthesizer lines moved closer and further away in a space by using reverb automation alone.

This is a technique that should be used sparingly but is effective in music genres that rely on a slow, steady evolution of the musical texture, like ambient or dub techno.

It can also be successfully combined with the more explosive tension-and-release drop technique mentioned earlier in this section.

In the next and final section, we'll explore the use of OTT/Multiband Dynamics to give your reverb tail a warped, otherworldly feel.

8.4: Upward Compression

There are many ways to go about experimenting with unusual reverberation. One of the easiest methods is to add compression effects to your reverb tail. This is done by adding a multiband upward/downward compressor to your auxiliary channel after the reverb plugin such as the free Xfer OTT plugin or—if you are using

Ableton—the OTT preset of Multiband Dynamics, as shown in Figure 8.36:

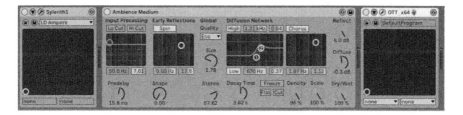

Figure 8.36: An effects chain with OTT added after the Reverb device.

OTT/Multiband Dynamics uses a technique called upward compression to boost the volume of quieter sounds (beneath a set threshold) within the tail. Rather than decay gracefully as expected, a reverb tail given sufficient upward compression will instead momentarily *increase* in intensity. This creates an odd, otherworldly sound.

To illustrate this effect, in Figure 8.37 the instrument has stopped playing halfway through the clip and we can see the normal behaviour of its reverb tail in the waveform:

Figure 8.37: A reverb tail before the use of OTT.

Following the application of OTT however, this same reverb tail has become dynamic and unnatural. Its new waveform is shown in Figure 8.38:

Figure 8.38: A reverb tail after the use of OTT.

To make use upward compression yourself, first add an OTT plugin after your reverb within your DAW.

Now you can begin adjusting your OTT plugin.

1. You can safely keep the *Depth* parameter at 100%, although you may wish to tweak this later after you've completed the rest of your workflow (see item 7. below).

2. *In Gain* and *Out Gain* define the level of the sound as it enters and then emerges from the plugin, so for the time being, these can also both be left at 100%.

3. *Time* specifies how long the effect lasts. Because you're looking for a slow-burn effect, experiment with values from 0% to 100%. You'll probably find that values above 100% decay too quickly to have a meaningful effect.

4. Because you're using upward compression to affect the reverb tail, you'll probably want to maximise the upward compression that occurs. To find the ideal amount I usually begin by changing *Upwd* to 200%, and then slowly decrease this number until it produces the effect I'm looking for.

5. The three bands in the centre of the plugin—shown in Figure 8.39—are the most important and display the level of sound entering the compressor.

The areas to the left of the black bands allow you to define the levels of sound that will receive upward compression. It can therefore be helpful to increase the threshold of upward compression of the mid-range by clicking and dragging the mid black band towards the right. It's worth taking extra care when doing this however, since this upward compression also applies to your sound *before* the reverb tail, meaning that the OTT will not only change the character of your tail, but also the character of the instruments that are being reverberated. (The exception to this is when you're working through an aux channel, in which case the compression will apply to your reverb tail only.)

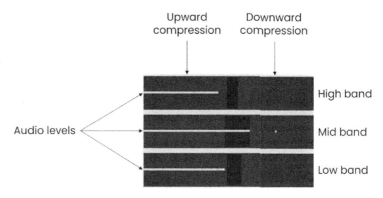

Figure 8.39: The three EQ bands that lie at the centre of OTT.

6. Finally, you can use the three EQ dials (H, M, and L) to the right of the bands to shape the overall frequency response of the plugin. When applying OTT to reverb, I favour

reducing the level of the low and high bands to emphasise the middling frequencies of the reverb tail, because this is the frequency range that adds the most body to your sound. An example of an OTT configuration required to achieve this is shown using Xfer's OTT plugin in Figure 8.40:

Figure 8.40: An example patch for adding upward compression to reverb.

7. To make the most of this upward compression, try adding extra audio information to your reverb tail. You can do this

by increasing its *Decay* time and introducing lots of treble and stereo information, as illustrated in Figure 8.41:

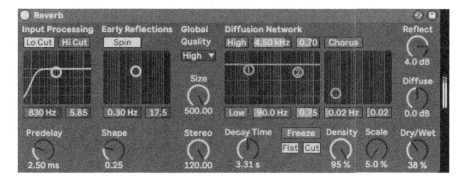

Figure 8.41: A bright reverb tail, created to exploit the warped effect that OTT creates.

8. Having fully set up your upward compression, you can now experiment with the *Depth* parameter to define the extent to which you want this effect to occur.

The entire configuration I've used here is shown below in Figure 8.42:

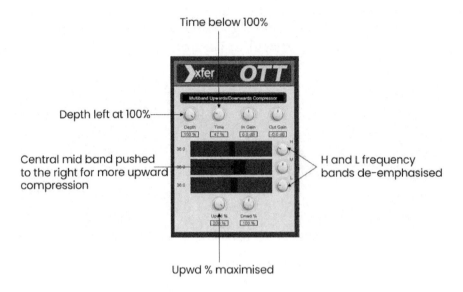

Time below 100%

Depth left at 100%

Central mid band pushed
to the right for more upward
compression

H and L frequency
bands de-emphasised

Upwd % maximised

Figure 8.42: An example OTT configuration.

The above configuration has produced a warped, multidirectional sound. If you wanted to create an even more unnatural sound, you could consider adding automated panning and distortion to this already-compressed reverb tail.

Alternatively, if you wanted more control over the reverb tail, you could record your OTT reverb tail and use it as a sample, which is effective when applied to chords and white noise stabs. It creates a fascinating dynamic that confounds the listener's expectations and draws them into the sound.

When used in the right context, the hints and tips provided in this chapter will take your use of reverb to the cutting edges of music production. You'll notice that they all combine the use of reverb with the use of an effect: reversing, gating, automation, and compression.

Cutoff: The frequency at which a filter rolls off – specifically when the filter has altered the level of the specified frequency by -3dB.

Damping: A filter applied to reverb over time to simulate the absorption of frequencies.

Delay: An effect created by layering delayed copies of a sound over itself. This creates echoes that gradually decay to nothing.

Density: Density refers to the 'thickness' of the reverb tail. This can be because of the number of echoes that occur within it, the distance between the early reflections and later reverb tail and sometimes a combination of the two.

Diffusion: Diffusion defines how the reverb tail is scattered around the hypothetical space. A highly diffused space will have more surfaces to bounce off and there will be a correspondingly higher number of echoes, resulting in a smooth reverb tail.

Digital: Music represented by capturing frames of audio using binary code.

****Dirt**: Lo-fi elements deliberately included in a recording.

Distortion: The alteration of the waveform. Can refer both to desirable clipping created by analog electronics, or unwanted clipping that negatively impacts sound quality.

Drop: A higher-energy section of a track. Often used to release the tension built up during a 'break'.

Dry: The unaltered signal in an effects unit. Can also describe a sound without reverb or delay effects added.

Dry/Wet: A selector that allows the user to mix Dry and Wet signals, determining the amount of unaltered signal allowed through an effects unit.

Ducking: The effect of a signal being intermittently pushed downwards by sidechain compression.

Dynamic Range: The difference between the loudest and quietest parts of a sound/track.

Dynamics: The differences in amplitude within a piece of audio.

Early Reflections: The initial part of a reverb tail, most commonly occurring during the first 5-25ms.

*****Envelope**: The shape of a sound, defined by its attack, decay, sustain and release (ADSR).

EQ: An effect that alters the levels of selected frequency bands.

Feedback: When an effect feeds the output of a signal into its input, exaggerating the effect.

Filter: An effect that only allows particular bands of frequency through.

Frequency: The number of waveform cycles per second. Correlates with pitch.

Fundamental Frequency: The lowest, and usually loudest, frequency of a musical note. This tends to be the note played, i.e., playing a G2 note on a piano will emit a fundamental frequency of G2. The fundamental frequency, combined with the harmonics created by the instrument, create the note's timbre.

FX: A shortened term for 'effects'.

Gain: A decrease or increase in the amplitude of a sound. Often forms part of an effects unit that may affect the amplitude of the sound, such as compression or distortion.

Gate: An effect that only allows audio signals above a certain threshold through.

Hall reverb: A reverb algorithm or preset designed to simulate an orchestral hall.

Harmonics: Frequencies that are integer multiples of the fundamental frequency.

Harmonic Distortion: Distortion that adds frequencies that bear a harmonic relationship to the sounds being distorted.

Hertz (Hz): A measure of frequency, referring to cycles per second.

High End: The upper levels of the frequency spectrum, usually those above 2kHz.

High Pass Filter: A filter that only allows frequencies above the cutoff through.

Impulse Response: The response of a system to a brief input (which is the 'impulse'). Often used to model the reverberant response of an environment (such as a particular room) or a device (such as a reverb plate).

Insert Effect: An effect placed upon a single channel.

Late Reflections: The second part of the reverb tail, after the early reflections have elapsed.

LFO: Low Frequency Oscillator. Is usually a modulation source, used for example to vary the frequency of a filter over time.

Limiter: A harsh form of compression that prevents sounds from breaching the threshold.

Lo-Fi: Low fidelity. A music production choice that includes imperfections in recording (or artificially introduces these imperfections to create atmosphere).

Loop: A repeated sequence of music.

Low-End: The lower levels of the frequency spectrum, generally those below 400Hz.

Low-Pass Filter: A filter that only allows frequencies below the cutoff through.

Mid-range: The middling range of frequencies, usually between 400Hz and 2kHz.

MIDI: A technical standard for electronic music instruments to interface with one another.

MIDI Controller: A hardware controller physically designed to manipulate MIDI parameters.

Mixer: A device that allows the producer to change the volume, EQ and dynamics of individual audio tracks.

Modulation: The change of a parameter by another source, for example an LFO or an envelope.

Mono: Not stereo, so the Left and Right channels are identical.

Oscillator: The component in an electronic device that generates a waveform at the selected frequency.

OTT: A preset of Ableton's Multiband Dynamics device that has been developed into its own plugin by Xfer Records.

Pan / Panning: The distribution of a track or audio within the stereo field.

Parameter: Any control on a device that can be manipulated.

Parametric Equalizer: A type of equaliser controlled by 'bands' that can be manipulated.

Patch: A saved combination of parameters that can be loaded to a plugin.

Peak: The part of a sound with the highest amplitude.

Phase: Where, in time, a waveform starts and repeats.

Pitch: The frequency of a musical note.

Plate Reverb: A reverb algorithm or preset designed to simulate the effects produced by a physical plate reverb device.

Plugin: A virtual audio device that can be added to a DAW to enhance its functions.

Polyphony: In music theory, polyphony is the simultaneous combination of two or more notes. When referring to synthesizers, it means the synthesizer can play more than one note at the same time.

Pot: A parameter controlled by rotating a knob, like the equalisers on a DJ mixer.

Preset: A combination of pre-established parameters that can be loaded into a plugin.

Process in Parallel: The processing of a sound at the same time as the original, for example using Dry/Wet.

Quantisation: A software function that moves MIDI notes to conform to the location of notes on a grid.

Resonance: A parameter on a filter that stresses the cutoff point.

Return Channel: An alternative term for an auxiliary channel.

Reverb Tail: The sum of the effect produced by reverberation, including both the early and late reflections.

Room Reverb: A reverb algorithm or preset designed to simulate a small room.

Sample: The re-use within a track of a section of previously recorded audio, usually taken from elsewhere. Can often refer to pieces of audio taken from another track, for example, the Amen Break.

Sample Rate: The number of snapshots of audio per second in a digital audio file.

Sampling: Taking audio from another track to use as a sample.

Send: A control that defines how much of a signal is sent to an auxiliary channel.

Sequencer: The function in a DAW (or hardware sequencer) that allows you to sequence MIDI and audio clips over time.

Sibilance: The amount of harsh 'S' sounds in a recording of a vocalist. Can often sound unpleasant.

Sidechain: A function, often found in a compressor, that can trigger an effects unit based on an external audio source.

Signal: Audio passing through a digital or analog circuit.

Slider: A parameter controlled by up and down or side to side movement, like the faders on a DJ mixer.

Spring Reverb: A reverb algorithm or preset designed to simulate a physical spring reverb device.

Stereo: A sound that contains both left and right channel information.

Stereo Image: The overall 'image' created by panning.

Subtractive Synthesis: A form of synthesis that starts with basic waveforms, then 'subtracts' from them using processors such as filters.

Tempo: The speed of a track.

Timbre: The characteristic texture of a sound. In acoustic music the harmonics created by an instrument are responsible for generating its recognisable timbre.

Track: Can refer to a finished piece of recorded music, or an individual channel within a DAW.

Transient: The initial, loud part of a sound, such as when a drummer first strikes a drum.

Velocity: A MIDI parameter, that is usually used to dictate the amplitude of a sound but can be routed to other parameters such as the filter frequency.

Vocoder: A device that combines frequency content with an external source (often vocals) to create a novel sound.

WAV File: A standard type of audio file.

Waveform: The graphical representation of an audio wave.

Wavetable Synthesis: A form of synthesis that starts with many different waveforms, then processes them.

Wet: A processed version of a signal, as opposed to the dry, unprocessed version.

Printed in Great Britain
by Amazon

42803346R00126